D0354131

MIRACLES &
MOMENTS
of GRACE

ALSO BY NANCY B. KENNEDY

Miracles & Moments of Grace:
Inspiring Stories from Military Chaplains

Miracles & Moments of Grace:
Inspiring Stories from Moms

Miracles & Moments of Grace:
Inspiring Stories of Survival

How We Did It:
Weight Loss Choices that Will Work for You!

Make It, Shake It, Mix It Up

Even the Sound Waves Obey Him

MIRACLES & MOMENTS of GRACE

INSPIRING STORIES FROM DOCTORS

BY NANCY B. KENNEDY

Guideposts

New York

This Guideposts edition is published by special arrangement with Leafwood Publishers, an imprint of Abilene Christian University Press.

MIRACLES & MOMENTS OF GRACE
INSPIRING STORIES FROM DOCTORS

LEAFWOOD
P U B L I S H E R S
an imprint of Abilene Christian University Press

Copyright 2012 by Nancy B. Kennedy

ISBN 978-0-89112-110-7
LCCN 2011052029

Printed in the United States of America

Scripture quotations, unless otherwise noted, are from The Holy Bible, New International Version. Copyright 1984, International Bible Society. Used by permission of Zondervan Publishers. Scripture quotations noted NLT are taken from the Holy Bible, New Living Translation, copyright 1996, 2004. Used by permission of Tyndale House Publishers, Inc., Wheaton, Illinois 60189. All rights reserved.

LIBRARY OF CONGRESS CATALOGING-IN-PUBLICATION DATA
Miracles & moments of grace : inspiring stories from doctors / [edited by] Nancy B. Kennedy.
    p. cm.
Includes bibliographical references and index.
ISBN 978-0-89112-110-7
 1. Medicine--Religious aspects--Christianity--Anecdotes. 2. Healing--Religious aspects-
-Christianity--Anecdotes. 3. Miracles--Anecdotes. 4. Physicians--United States--Biography. I.
Kennedy, Nancy B. II. Title: Miracles and moments of grace.
 BT732.M57 2012
 261.5'61--dc23

                                                                          2011052029

Cover design by ThinkPen Design, Inc.

Published in association with William K. Jensen Literary Agency,
119 Bampton Court, Eugene, Oregon 97404

Leafwood Publishers is an imprint of
Abilene Christian University Press
ACU Box 29138
Abilene, Texas 79699
1-877-816-4455

For current information about all Leafwood titles, visit our Website:
www.leafwood publishers.com

20 19 18 17 16 15 14 13 12 11 10 9 8 7 6 5 4 3 2 1

For those on whom misfortune has fallen—

I would pray for you a doctor such as these.

Table of Contents

Introduction

When you find yourself in that chilly exam room gowned in a flimsy blue paper robe and balanced uneasily on that high exam table, have you ever wondered what is going on in the mind of the doctor perched on that low stool in front of you?

I wish I could say that I have had lofty thoughts of this nature. But, to be honest, I'm generally too wrapped up in worry about my own puny self to give my doctor the barest of thoughts. I want a diagnosis! I want a pill! I want to feel better, and I want to feel better *now*. "The patient does not care about your science; what he wants to know is, can you cure him?" said Martin H. Fischer, a doctor and author of the mid-1900s.[1] He's sure got that right.

But after writing this book, all that has changed.

For my first book in the Miracles & Moments of Grace series, I told the gripping and inspiring stories of our nation's military chaplains. I followed the chaplains from their domestic assignments to their deployments, from peacetime into war, from brief moments of tenderness to scenes of unbearable tragedy.

For a year, I worked with my chaplains' stories on an almost daily basis. Yet it didn't matter how many times I visualized the events in my head—to me, every time I read those stories was like reading them for the first time. I was swept up in my chaplains' drama. I was brought to tears by their sorrows. I was horrified by the dangers they faced and awed by their deep knowledge of human and divine nature.

Without a doubt, the year I spent with my chaplains was one of the most personally satisfying years of my writing life. Getting to know those valiant and spiritually vibrant men and women added a rich spiritual and personal dimension to my life.

So when the idea for telling stories from our nation's doctors came up, I was eager to return to my storytelling role. I envisioned the situations doctors might face through the years—situations in which life and death are as intricately entwined as my chaplains' experiences were. And, just as I found my chaplains to be warm, thoughtful, and sensitive human beings, I anticipated that my doctors would be, too.

It was no surprise to me when my suspicions turned out to be true. After talking with the fifty doctors who tell their stories in this book, I have to say: There's plenty going on inside your doctor's head! And I wanted to hear every single thought they had. I considered it an immense privilege to be granted this fleeting look into the inner lives of these inspiring men and women of medicine.

The wonderful stories you are about to read open a window into the preparation for and the practice of medicine. They come from some of the most insightful human beings on the face of the earth. Time and again, I found myself praying that when the occasion inevitably arises, any one of these physicians be the doctor I face in that stark exam room.

Before talking with my doctors, it seemed to me that patients— patients like me!—stand in awe of their doctors, even today when it has become our habit to self-diagnose and self-medicate via the Internet. I have heard a doctor's work called a "pedestal profession" because of the high regard in which doctors are held. And, from my perspective, given a doctor's intimate knowledge of the workings of the human body with all its mysteries and complexities, I believe doctors should make themselves comfortable up there on that pedestal.

I was filled with awe listening to the stories of these skilled men and women who know how to diagnose, how to treat—how even to cut open a living person and repair what's gone wrong, no matter how demanding or how delicate the task. Having only a meager liberal arts degree to my name, I'd find myself thinking: *Do they really know how to do that?*

But as I talked to my doctors, I found that more often than not it was the doctors themselves who expressed awe for their patients. Repeatedly, doctors told me tales of gaining inspiration from their patients and from the experiences these patients shared with them, allowing them to become that caring, listening soul sharing the exam room with you.

Doctors are busy people, their days long and their leisure hours brief. So, when I asked them about their experiences, I kept my inquiries short and to the point. Most often, I simply asked, "What is the one moment that remains in your mind as the most memorable moment of your career?" Almost every doctor could pinpoint immediately the one incident that was so deeply meaningful they could describe it down to the smallest detail, whether it happened yesterday or many years in the past.

In his book, *How We Age,* Dr. Marc E. Agronin, a geriatric psychiatrist, speaks eloquently about this moment. He was the catalyst for restoring health to an 85-year-old man, a Holocaust survivor whose illness had seemed, on the surface, incurable, an inevitable result of the aging process. But it turned out not to be true. Dr. Agronin's diligent exploration—based on his intuition that the simplest diagnosis is not always the correct one—reversed the course of a seemingly hopeless situation. He describes the gratitude he felt at being chosen for this life-affirming experience:

I was one small part of a transcendent chain of events, a
messenger sent on a preordained mission. In every doctor's
life there should be at least one such moment of satisfaction.
. . . This was my moment, and I shall never forget it.[2]

Because of these experiences—experiences of unexpected healings,
of divinely appointed chance, or even of the tragic deaths of their
patients—doctors often find themselves forever changed.

These moments may thrill doctors, or puzzle them, or make them
challenge their conception of themselves, but they are so universal
that almost every doctor who has taken up the pen tries to make sense
of them. Author and brain surgeon Allan Hamilton, MD, addresses
how these transcendent moments have touched his life:

I always wished someone had said that you are going to see
stuff that is going to make you question your values. You are
going to question yourself, and that is part of medicine and
part of taking care of human beings. Maybe it is the mystery
of taking care of life.[3]

Surgeon John Fulginiti III, one of the doctors you'll meet in this book,
has thought deeply about the mystery of caring for life. He has seen
the many ways our physical selves can fail us and has encountered
many cases in which he could not restore health, no matter how much
he wished to do so. But Dr. Fulginiti, a deeply spiritual person, does
not consider even the worst outcome to negate the divine intentions
of our Creator. "As doctors, we see the disorder of creation, the nature
of our fallen world, but it does not overcome God and his beauty," Dr.
Fulginiti says. "We are finite creatures, but death does not have the
final say."

Like Dr. Fulginiti, Robert Paeglow, MD, the founder of a free clinic in a poor area of Albany, New York, has seen his share of human misery. But he has also experienced miracles of healing that he says are too numerous to count. In light of that, he has made a firm resolve never to lose hope.

"I will never bow and worship at the altar of despair and cynicism," Dr. Paeglow says. When you read his story in this book, you'll see why he has made this vow to himself.

These moments seemed to come upon many doctors in the midst of their careers, after years of the daily practice of medicine. They'd seen thousands of patients and faced almost every situation imaginable, but suddenly their attention was grabbed by a divinely granted thought or an inexplicable urge to act.

But many times, these life-altering moments came early in a doctor's career, while they were still in medical school or completing an internship or residency program. These years of training are a formative time, a time when the enormity of their undertaking presses on young doctors, but also a time when they are imprinted with vivid experiences that fill them with wonder and affirm them in their path as healers.

One such doctor is Sidney Barnes III, MD, a surgeon at Atlantic General Hospital in Berlin, Maryland. During his residency in a New Jersey hospital, Dr. Barnes was once called to the emergency room for a patient who was bleeding out from a neck wound.

Dr. Barnes arrived in the ER to find a man in his early 70s whose wound was pulsating blood from the carotid artery, the vital artery that supplies blood to the brain.

The patient had undergone extensive treatment for a cancer in his neck, both chemotherapy and radiation. Neither treatment had been successful. Now, the cancer had advanced so thoroughly as to erode the carotid artery.

The attending physician that night had been treating this gentleman for years; in fact, they were personal friends. He staunched the bleeding with a dressing and sat down at his friend's side. In a gentle but straightforward way, he laid out the options before him and his wife.

"Dan, the most aggressive treatment would be for us to operate on you now, tie off the artery and repair the damage as best we can," he said.

"If we do," he continued, "there is a good chance you will have a stroke and die during the operation. If you do survive, sometime down the road you will most likely find yourself in the same situation you are in now.

"Our other option," he said, "is to let you bleed out now. I can assure you that bleeding to death is not painful. With the loss of blood, you would simply go to sleep. . . . I want to give you time to think this over, and I want you to know that whatever option you choose, I will do my best for you."

Having given his friend this information, the attending physician and Dr. Barnes stepped out of the room to allow Dan and his wife to talk privately. Ten minutes later, the couple called the doctors back in.

"We want to go with the second option," Dan said.

Having thus decided, Dan and his wife proceeded to call all of their children, their children's spouses, and their grandchildren to the hospital. One by one, this beloved father and grandfather took each into his room to say a last goodbye.

Despite the knowledge of his coming death, Dan was calm and even jovial. He joked with his children and grandchildren, and they couldn't help but laugh with him. He told them how much they meant to him and that he loved them. Each family member hugged and kissed him before they left his room.

"I'll see you on the other side," he said to them as they left.

Finally, Dan and his wife were left alone together in the room. Some minutes passed while the couple said their final, tender good-byes. Then, Dan called the doctors back in.

"You've been a good friend, doc. I love you," he said to the attending physician. "Thank you for everything you've done for us.

"I'm ready now."

With that, the attending physician removed the man's dressing from his neck, and in just a few minutes he bled out, dying quietly and peacefully, just as the doctor had promised.

This patient's courage in the face of death made a lasting impression on the young Dr. Barnes. *If I were in his shoes, could I have made that decision?* he wondered. *Could I have said my goodbyes so calmly and lovingly?*

This encounter spoke to Dr. Barnes mightily about the infinite value of both living well and dying well. More broadly, though, and just as memorably, it spoke to him about becoming the kind of doctor who, like this attending physician, could be a calm and reassuring guide for a fellow human being facing the impending call of death.

Incredible as Dr. Barnes's story is, it is an entirely true story, one of two he told me for this book. Likewise, all of the stories you will read in this book are absolutely true. In most cases, the doctors and I have changed the names of their patients, their friends and family, or of their colleagues to protect their privacy and the confidentiality of their stories. In a few instances, doctors chose to alter an identifying detail of a story, such as a medical diagnosis, in cases where the true information might easily identify a patient. But beyond that, nothing about the stories is fictional. Some of the doctors told their own stories, having written books, articles, or blogs, which I adapted for the book. In other cases, I interviewed the doctors and told their stories in their own words.

Dr. Sherwin B. Nuland, a surgeon and an award-winning author, once offered an explanation of why doctors—doctors who are busy enough already, who barely have the time to write prescriptions—take the time to tell their stories:

> I'm a surgeon who has been at this calling for a very long time, and even the least introspective of us cannot escape without having developed an entire steamer trunkful of experiences, impressions, philosophies and musings on the human condition, values and ethics.[4]

I am grateful to have had the opportunity to open a few of these steamer trunks and allow these fascinating stories to unfold before you.

NANCY B. KENNEDY
MARCH 2012

Cure sometimes,
treat often,
comfort always.

—Hippocrates

1

A Mother's Love

Ron Eaker, MD, FACOG

Obstetrics and Gynecology

Augusta, Georgia

The late, great philosopher and hunka-hunka burnin' love, Elvis, once sang a tune called "Blue Christmas." It was a hit largely because it resonated with all those who feel depressed during the holidays. Feeling blue over the holidays is epidemic—some studies indicate that more than 30 percent of the population suffers from this seasonal malady.

I will never forget the beautiful 18-year-old I cared for one Thanksgiving in the emergency room. She had slashed her wrists with a razor blade and barely made it to the ER alive. Yet she did survive, and over the next several days, I got to know her better. I finally asked her why she had tried to take her life. She said simply, "I had no hope."

But every year around the holidays, I also find myself remembering Lisa. Her story is one of hope rather than hopelessness.

I first saw Lisa in the afternoon on Christmas Eve. She had been in labor for about eight hours. I had never met her before—I was on call for our practice and just coming on duty. She was only halfway there, and it was obvious from looking at her why it is called labor. Sweat was rolling off her brow, and her expression was one of fear, expectation, and pain all wrapped up together.

She continued to progress, each contraction harder than the previous one. Her breathing became panting, and those little beads of sweat became a drenching shower of effort. I would periodically pop in to check her progress, and each time I noted her resolve and quiet determination. She knew that her pain was all for a greater purpose.

As she came closer to delivery, Lisa reached the state known as transition. This is often the stage of labor where Miss Manners' decorum is utterly abandoned! She negotiated these final minutes heroically, pushed effectively, and delivered a beautiful baby girl.

Almost immediately, I noticed a problem with the baby's eyes—they were widely spaced, more so than normal. Then I saw her clubfoot. When I examined her further, it became obvious that this beautiful baby girl had Down syndrome.

As I carried this newly swaddled baby over to her eager mother, I struggled with how to tell her of my suspicions. The moment of a child's birth is such an emotional event, the moment most parents consider the highlight of their lives. Hearing this news can feel like a slap in the face. In their fear and confusion, a new parent doesn't even know how to react.

I said a quick prayer and decided to be forthright. As I laid the infant on Lisa's belly, I gently placed my hand on her shoulder and told her I thought the baby had Down syndrome. Then I showed her the baby's clubfoot.

Lisa paused for what seemed like an eternity, her eyes never leaving her baby. Finally, she spoke.

"Isn't God great!" she said.

That caught me totally off guard. It was definitely not the response I had expected. Then she continued:

"God knew to send this baby to someone who would love her just as she is," she said.

With that, Lisa drew her left arm out from under the bedsheets. For the first time, I saw that Lisa's own arm and hand were deformed, her fingers fused and malformed.

When a child is born, parents bristle with the joy of unbridled hope. Hope for their child's health, hope for their future, hope for a life of meaning and purpose. Sometimes those hopes are dashed. But just as two thousand years ago the birth of a baby boy to a young mother in a shabby horse stall was a portent of hope, the birth of this baby was an amazing source of hope and joy for Lisa. Yes, God is indeed good and wise.

Dr. J. Ron Eaker is a board-certified obstetrician and gynecologist. He is a Fellow in the American College of Obstetricians and Gynecologists and a clinical advisor to the American Running and Fitness Association. Dr. Eaker is the author of several books, including Healthy Habits for a Fit Family *(Revell, 2011) and* A Woman's Guide to Hormone Health *(Bethany House, 2009). He and his wife, Susan, have two daughters, Katie and Caroline.*

2

PRAYER AND A LITTLE BRIBERY

JOHN CROPSEY, MD

OPHTHALMOLOGY

BOMET, KENYA

My trip to Sudan was the stuff dreams are made of. Some of them are my own silly dreams, like operating in the middle of nowhere in blazing heat, barefoot, and dressed only in shorts, T-shirt, baseball cap, and sterile gloves.

Our team went to the southern village of Akot, in the middle of this war-torn land, to hold a week-long eye clinic. When we landed at the airstrip, we were greeted by a blast of 100-plus degree heat and a group of enthusiastic boys, one wielding an AK-47—the airstrip happens to share space with an army barracks, along with the clinic that was going to be our base for the week.

Despite the violence of the area, and the sound of nearby gunfire the first three nights, God brought plenty of people to the clinic. Before we'd left for Sudan, we had put together a team of people from all over the world praying that we would be able to perform 100 surgeries in just six days.

Those who were blinded by cataracts, glaucoma, trachoma, retinal disease, and other conditions were led to the clinic by a family member, often a small child as young as four or five years old. The child holds onto one end of a stick, and the blind person follows by holding onto the other end.

By the end of the week, we had indeed completed 100 surgeries, and we thought we were finished. We had prayed for 100 patients, after all! But just as we were finishing up, a four-year-old boy arrived with his father. The boy, Marial, had suffered an injury to his right eye from a stick, causing a traumatic cataract with a scarred corneal laceration. We would have to operate.

We had no anesthesia to offer except a local injection, so Marial would have to be awake for the procedure. The surgery would take about 40 minutes, and it was imperative that he remain absolutely still the entire time. The slightest movement could mean a disastrous outcome. Marial said he understood he would have to be very still.

After much prayer and a little bribery—a bottle of Coke and a candy bar!—Marial allowed us to administer the retrobulbar block, and we began.

We sterilized Marial's eye with an iodine solution and placed a sterile surgical drape over his head with a hole centered over his wounded eye. I made an incision on the sclera, the white part of the eye, and then tunneled up into his cornea in order to extract the cataract that was positioned just behind the iris, the colored part of the eye. Finally, I slipped an artificial plastic lens into the eye in place of the cataract.

Marial was an absolute angel! He did not move during the entire surgery. But as I placed my last suture, he suddenly and utterly broke down, sobbing and thrashing around, his pent-up fear and anxiety unleashing all at once. If that had happened a few minutes earlier, it surely would have been a disaster.

Marial was admitted to the clinic overnight, and I checked on him before we boarded the bush plane. Everything looked great—the surgery had been a success. We left medicines for our eye patients with the clinic doctor and then headed back to Kenya.

Upon our return to Kenya, I was having dinner with the other eye doctor who had gone on the trip, when his wife told me something surprising. She said that on the last day of our clinic, she had been burdened to pray that before we left, a young boy would come out of the Sudanese bush for the eye care that he needed.

When I heard that, I was thrilled! The Holy Spirit had moved a team of people from all over the world to pray for us. He had moved a woman to pray for a little boy she did not know and Marial's father to bring his son to the clinic. He had empowered Marial to keep perfectly still and me to accomplish the surgery. The way God orchestrated so many events in so many places to bring healing to Marial was awe-inspiring for me to experience.

"We don't believe in miracles—we depend on them," my dad, a missionary doctor himself, told us many, many times. This has been proven true a million times over by medical missionaries around the globe, century after century. All I can say is: thank you for your prayers.

Dr. John Cropsey was an ophthalmologist at the Eye Unit of Tenwek Hospital in Bomet, Kenya, as part of a two-year post-residency program with Samaritan's Purse. He grew up in Togo, West Africa, where his father was a surgeon and his mother a nurse at a rural mission hospital. He and his wife, Jessica, have two children, Elise and Micah. "Prayer and a Little Bribery" is adapted with permission from the blog post "Sudan on a Wing and a Prayer" from the blog Word and Deed (www.mccropders.blogspot.com).

3

A HOLY BREATH

PETER GREENSPAN, DO, FACOG, FACS

OBSTETRICS AND GYNECOLOGY

KANSAS CITY, MISSOURI

I was in private practice in Independence, Missouri, when I was called on to attend a patient of mine who was in labor.

This was a mother who had undergone a Caesarean section for her first childbirth. For her second child, she wanted to attempt a vaginal birth. VBAC—vaginal birth after Caesarean—was a fairly controversial idea then, and not many doctors were comfortable with it. It carries some substantial risks, and if complications ensue, it can be catastrophic for both mother and baby.

My patient's labor continued for a number of hours, maybe six or eight, and it was hard labor. But she wasn't making any progress, and I was concerned about the length of time that had passed, so I recommended a C-section. The mother consented and preparation for the surgery began.

To ensure the health of the mother and baby, you want to start a C-section within a half hour of when the decision is made. So, after a C-section has been decided on, about a dozen things happen quickly and all at once. A crew is called in to prepare the operating room.

Professionals converge from all around the hospital—a surgeon and an assistant, an anesthesiologist, scrub nurses, circulating nurses, the surgical technician who ensures that equipment is working properly, personnel to revive the baby if that becomes necessary, and nursery nurses to care for the baby.

This time was no different. There was a swirl of activity around me, but there was no sense of urgency. This wasn't an emergency situation. We were just efficiently going about our preparations for the surgery.

I watched the proceedings as I scrubbed up in the hallway outside the OR. Through the OR window, I could see people scurrying about as the operating room was prepared. On the other side of the hall, I noted the growing commotion surrounding the mother.

Suddenly, I felt what I can only describe as a holy wind on the back of my neck. It wasn't a voice; no one said anything. It was just the sensation of breath on my neck. In that instant, an urgent thought bore down on me: *I have to deliver this baby right now.*

I strode into the operating room, as though propelled by a hand pushing me from behind.

As a nurse gowned me, I said to her, "Give me a knife. I have to start right away." It was my call—no one questioned me.

The operation began, and within a minute I had a clear view of my patient's uterus. It had ruptured.

A ruptured uterus is life threatening. A laboring mother can die from this complication. She is in danger of going into shock and cardiac arrest from blood loss. Often, the only way to save the mother's life is a Caesarean hysterectomy, which will render a young woman incapable of getting pregnant again.

Equally as heartbreaking is that upwards of 75 percent of the babies die. It is a bloody job to deliver a baby under these conditions, and if too much time passes, the baby can bleed out or suffer irreparable brain damage. You only have a few minutes.

From the looks of it, my patient's rupture had occurred just a few minutes earlier. Still, the damage was already spreading. The baby was immersed in the contents of the uterus that had spilled out into the abdominal cavity, and the mother was hemorrhaging. In addition, the patient's bladder had ruptured where the uterus and bladder meet.

Quickly, I extracted the baby. I swung around and handed the baby back to the nurses and then turned back to my patient. After we delivered the placenta, I managed to stop the bleeding and repair the damage to the uterus and the bladder.

Throughout the procedure, an aura of calm reigned, despite the circumstances. There were a lot of people in the operating room, and now we were working urgently, but the coordination of efforts couldn't have been finer. The C-section was a success. Both mother and baby lived and were fine.

As a believer, I feel blessed all the time, but that moment—that breath of wind on my neck—was a truly spiritual moment. I know it was the presence of the Holy Spirit, the *Ru'akh ha Kodesh* that I knew from my Jewish upbringing. I take no credit for the outcome of that surgery. To God be all the glory.

Dr. Peter Greenspan practices obstetrics and gynecology at Lakewood Medical Center in Lakewood, Missouri. He is a Fellow in the American College of Obstetricians and Gynecologists and in the American College of

Surgeons. He is associate chairman for the Department of Obstetrics and Gynecology at the University of Missouri–Kansas City School of Medicine, where he is also an associate professor and associate program director. He and his wife, Kathryn, have four children, David, Aliya, Lauren, and Matthew.

4

THIS FLEETING HOPE

RANDY CHRISTENSEN, MD

PEDIATRIC MEDICINE

PHOENIX, ARIZONA

In my years of providing medical care to homeless children, I've learned to celebrate the successes—the kids who find a way out of their self-destructive path—because all too often it doesn't end that way.

Nick arrived at our mobile medical clinic one day looking for treatment. He came aboard the converted Winnebago we affectionately call "Big Blue" needing medication for his asthma. Our van is outfitted with three exam rooms and all the medical equipment and medicines we need for treating the wide array of conditions we see in street kids. We park the van at regular stops in the poorer neighborhoods of Phoenix and the surrounding area.

Nick didn't look like a homeless young person. He looked like any of the thousands of college kids we see around here—jeans, a clean polo shirt, nice shoes. His hair was short and styled neatly. When he talked, he sounded like an educated young man. I was impressed by his vocabulary and his nuanced way of thinking.

Unlike many kids we see, Nick came from a pretty wealthy family that lived in a southeastern state. He denied suffering any abuse in his childhood home and didn't harbor any hatred for his family, as many abused or neglected children do.

But like so many other kids, Nick had a drug habit. Although he faithfully took the asthma medication we gave him, he continued to use drugs while we treated him. Every chance I could, I'd urge him to stop using.

"You've got to stop," I told him. "You're playing a game of Russian roulette. Every time you use, it's like you've loaded a bullet into the chamber of a gun, and it's spinning around. Unless you stop, the drugs are going to kill you."

At these words, Nick would bristle.

"Yes, I know it," he'd say curtly. "But I'm not going to stop." Like so many kids, he probably thought it wouldn't happen to him, or maybe he just didn't care if it did.

Gwen was a similarly likeable young woman. She first came to our clinic at one of our regular stops in Tempe near the Arizona State campus. She was a pretty girl, about five feet tall and slender. She was totally enveloped in a huge Army jacket. She wasn't tough, as many street kids are. She was lively and cheerful, and despite her soft demeanor, she was clearly a leader. She came in trailing an entourage of followers.

Unlike Nick, however, Gwen came from a rough background. Every member of her family was addicted to drugs, and not just her immediate family, but also her extended family—her stepmother, her mother's boyfriend, her aunts, her uncles, and her grandparents. Even so, on the outside she seemed unaffected by the tragedy of her family, always joking and laughing with our staff.

I could see Gwen was incredibly smart, and not just in the way that kids need to be smart in order to survive the hardships and violence of the streets. She liked to talk literature with me in a depth that went beyond a superficial "Have you read any Mark Twain?" kind of banter. I minored in poetry in medical school, so I was happy to discuss books and poems with her.

As Gwen filled out our intake form, I was astounded by her history of drug use. She checked off every single substance we listed and stated that her drug use started at the age of eight or nine years old.

Gwen had come for the complete blood workup we offer. In a child with a drug history such as hers, I was almost certain I'd find the usual diseases—HIV, AIDS, Hepatitis C, sexually transmitted diseases, or liver and kidney damage. Incredibly, despite her risky behaviors, Gwen's lab work came back free of disease.

But I knew that for Gwen—as for so many others like her—it was only a matter of time.

One thing I've learned while running this medical van is not to ask after the kids who stop coming to us. There's never a good reason for it, and I can't bear to hear that they might be dead. Nick stopped coming after two years. Gwen disappeared after just a few months.

Nick and Gwen haunt me because they were young people with so much potential. I really liked them both and desperately wanted a different outcome for them. I had hoped they would be among the fortunate ones who find their way out of their impoverished circumstances. I see a few of these kids occasionally when I'm out running errands—drug-free, holding down jobs, married, raising a family.

But most of the time we're just planting seeds. Yes, we're caring for these kids' bodies, but we're also holding out hope for a better life, if only for a moment.

When people ask me why I do what I do, it's because I want to plant these seeds. I grew up in a family that knew the value of this fleeting hope. We weren't poor, but we lived paycheck to paycheck. Even so, my dad was quick to help neighbors with their cars and home repairs. My mom saved up all our loose change in a piggy bank and at Christmastime shook it all out and gave it to someone in need. It couldn't have been more than 25 dollars each time, but it was all she had, and she gave it gladly.

As each child leaves our clinic, I think to myself, *Maybe we planted a seed in this one.* Maybe we did, and maybe the future will change for some of these kids. That is the hope that fuels the crew of Big Blue and keeps our wheels rolling.

Dr. Randy Christensen is the medical staff president and division chief of Pediatric and Adolescent Medicine at Phoenix Children's Hospital, and the medical director of the hospital's Crews'n Healthmobile, which provides healthcare services to homeless and at-risk children, adolescents, and young adults with two mobile medical units and a fixed-site clinic at the UMOM New Day Centers in Phoenix, Arizona. Dr. Christensen wrote about the mobile clinic in Ask Me Why I Hurt: The Kids Nobody Wants and The Doctor Who Heals Them *(Broadway Books, 2011). He and his wife, Amy, who is also a pediatrician for the Crews'n Healthmobile, have three children, Jane, Reed, and Charlotte.*

5

A Night Long Ago

James Avery, MD, FACP, FACCP, FAAHPM
Chief Executive Officer
Hospice of the Piedmont
Charlottesville, Virginia

Although the world is full of suffering,
it is also full of the overcoming of it.
Helen Keller

Many years ago, I was in private practice as a family physician. One of my patients was a very sick man. He was suffering from emphysema and chronic obstructive pulmonary disease. I saw George with his wife for several years, treating him for his breathing difficulties and other symptoms.

In time, I closed my practice and became the medical director of a local community hospice. One day, George came to me and told me his doctors had said he had just six months to live. He asked if I would again be his physician, and of course, I agreed.

George's case was among the hardest I'd encountered as a doctor. He was constantly short of breath and struggling for air. He did not want to live out his life in the hospital, so it became my goal just to keep him out of it.

But the most puzzling thing was that George seemed to be suffering beyond his diagnoses. His shortness of breath was worse than I would have expected to see. He was restless at night, shouting out in his sleep and waking continually. Nothing we did for him, not even sleep medication and strong narcotics, helped. He and his wife were exhausted, unable to get even one good night of sleep.

One day, looking for answers, I visited George at his home. The couple greeted me and led me into their living room. Again, we tackled the sleeping problem.

"Why aren't the sleeping pills working? Do you have any idea?" I asked him once more.

George paused before answering. It was a very long pause. And then, quietly, he asked his wife to leave the room.

My goodness, I thought. *What's this all about?* My first thought was that George was going to admit to some sort of infidelity, maybe an affair from some years back. People frequently confessed personal failures to me as they entered the last phase of their life.

After his wife had left the room, I waited for him to begin.

When George finally spoke, he was in obvious distress. His words came out slowly, so slowly and with so much difficulty that I thought he was going to stop at any minute. Every word was an agony for him. The distortion of his expression was as if with every word an ax were chopping at his heart.

Fifty years ago, George said haltingly, he was stationed with the Army during World War II on an island in the South Pacific. He'd had a tough war. He had endured hand-to-hand combat and watched many of his buddies die unspeakably horrible deaths.

One night, he was out on patrol in a jeep. George rounded a bend and, without warning, he came face-to-face with a company of about 30 Japanese soldiers. They were holding their weapons high in the air, lofting white flags in surrender.

George stopped the jeep, and without hesitation, he picked up a machine gun and mowed them all down.

With desperation in his eyes, George looked up at me.

I was stunned. *So this was why he was in such agony.* I was young and new to hospice, too inexperienced to know how to respond. Naïvely, I counseled him to forget his deed.

"You were young—it was war," I said, in a forgiving tone. "It was a long time ago."

"I . . . am . . . a murderer!" he answered in despair.

Suddenly, I realized that for his entire adult life, George had seen himself as a murderer. For fifty years, he had kept his secret. He had never said a word to anyone. He had never sought help from the military, never told his wife and family. All this time, he had suffered alone.

What a tremendous amount of courage it had taken for George to face his deed at last! I asked George if I could share his story with our hospice chaplain and his pastor, and he agreed. I prayed with him before I left.

With the help of his pastor and the hospice chaplain, it wasn't long before George gained the courage to tell his wife. Of course, she knew all along that something was wrong. She had felt a wall come up whenever the war was mentioned. Now she finally understood how drained her husband had been by the emotional energy it took to keep his secret.

Two weeks later, George called his two sons to his home to tell them his story. We sat in the living room once again. It was perhaps even more difficult for him to face his sons. When each of them was born, he told them, he had to leave the hospital and go home alone to cry, thinking about all the Japanese children who were never born because of what he did.

George's sons reacted spontaneously, with a lot of hugging, tears, and words of forgiveness. In telling his story, George's fear of being found out was released, and he felt love and acceptance for the first time in his life since that terrifying night so long ago.

After that, bathed in the relief of love and forgiveness, George was far more comfortable. He slept restfully and suffered less from his symptoms. He died peacefully about a month later.

From George, I learned that every hospice patient—every person—needs forgiveness. Often, when people are younger, they suffer because of things that people have done to them. But at the end of life, whether people are young or old, it is the other way around. People want forgiveness for things they have done or things they haven't done, words they have spoken or words they should have spoken.

It is a universal truth that we all need forgiveness. It transcends all cultures. Now, when I counsel hospice patients, I tell them there are five things they need to say to their loved ones. They are five things that we all need to hear:

> Please forgive me.
> I forgive you.
> Thank you.
> I love you.
> Good-bye.

Dr. James Avery is chief executive officer of Hospice of the Piedmont in Charlottesville, Virginia. He was in private practice for 14 years before he became involved in hospice care. He is a Fellow in the American College of Physicians, a Fellow in the American College of Chest Physicians, and a Fellow in the American Academy of Hospice and Palliative Medicine. He and his wife, Jan, have three children, Jonathan, Joseph, and Juli.

Dr. Avery credits Ira Byock, MD, for learning these "Five Things." They come from his book, *Dying Well: The Prospect for Growth at the End of Life* (New York: Riverhead, 1997).

6

You're Tellin' Me!

VALERIE WALKER, MD

FAMILY MEDICINE

FLORISSANT, MISSOURI

One day, I saw a new patient's name on my schedule, a 58-year-old African American male who had asked for a physical.

I entered the exam room and introduced myself. My patient, Mr. JB, was about 5 feet, 6 inches tall and weighed 280 pounds. All you could see was his stomach! He told me he was a preacher. He had a small congregation, only 30 or so people, mostly family members. So, to supplement his income, he worked nights as a security guard at an office building. All in all, he led a pretty sedentary life.

As I proceeded with the physical, Mr. JB told me some of his health problems. They were the usual ones you'd associate with obesity— high blood pressure, lower back pain, acid reflux, and sleep apnea. He came to my office after chest pains had landed him in the emergency room.

More than that, though, I suspected that Mr. JB was depressed. He admitted to me that he thought his wife didn't love him anymore. For one thing, because of the sleep apnea, he had to use a CPAP machine and wear a mask to breathe at night.

"My wife is afraid of me! She says I look like an alien," he said sadly.

Mr. JB's wife had gone so far as to take out a life insurance policy on him, using her own money to buy it. She was pretty sure he was going to keel over any second, and she wanted some financial security! I think Mr. JB was a little scared himself.

"Doctor Walker, if this ol' gray mule is gone, who's gonna pull the cart?" he asked me in despair.

When I completed the physical, I gave him my assessment of his situation. If nothing changed, I warned him, not only would his current conditions worsen, but he was at risk for many more serious problems—diabetes, osteoarthritis, and heart troubles, to name just a few.

"Your weight is causing most of your problems," I told him. "If you want to feel better, you'll have to deal with your weight."

Mr. JB said he'd try to do whatever I said. "Jesus didn't have a weight problem," he said. "So I'm not going to have a weight problem either."

I started in on my list of healthy habits. No smoking or drinking—that was easy; he didn't indulge in either. Cut down on salt, choose lean meats, fruits and vegetables instead of fried and fatty foods, reduce meal portions, and get some low-impact exercise like walking or water aerobics.

Mr. JB had just one question:

"When I work my night shifts, I snack on hard-boiled eggs," he said. "Isn't that healthy? I just salt 'em and pop 'em in my mouth, maybe a dozen a shift."

"Good heavens!" I cried. "That has got to stop!" And I filled him in on a few facts about cholesterol.

At the end of the exam, I asked Mr. JB to repeat back to me what he'd heard me say. I often do that with patients, just to see whether they've understood me correctly.

"Well now, Doctor," he said in his best preacher's voice. "You're telling me . . . that I'm reduced to boiled skinless chicken breasts and celery.

"You're tellin' me to salt just the outskirts of my food.

"You're tellin' me that if my food is delicious, spit it out!

"You're tellin' me that workin' the remote don't count as exercise.

"You're tellin' me that my best apple is, in fact, a pear!" he concluded emphatically.

Well, I let that last one slide, but on the whole, I could see he was getting the idea.

Over the next few months, Mr. JB made some progress. I could see that he was taking off some weight and feeling better. But not all of his complaints were gone.

"Doctor Walker, my wife is upset with you," he said one day. "Because of you, I'm still here. Now my wife is angry that she wasted all her money on that ol' insurance policy!"

Dr. Valerie Walker is board certified in family medicine and has a practice in Florissant, Missouri. She practices traditional, holistic, and spiritual healing methods. She hosts the television show House Calls *with Dr. Valerie Walker, aired by ABC30 (KDNL) in St. Louis, Missouri; WSIU/ WUSI in Carbondale, Illinois; KOZK in Springfield, Missouri; and KMOS in Warrensburg, Missouri. Dr. Walker has published a book of practical health and fitness tips titled* 131 Ways to Live 131 Years *(Brown Books, 2010), and she blogs about health at www.drvaleriewalker.com.*

7

A New Beginning

David Levy, MD

Neurosurgery

San Diego, California

An air of tension greeted me when I entered the exam room. As a neurosurgeon who specializes in aneurysms, I often see distressed patients who convey their worry through coldness, impatience, or anger.

Talia was a slender, attractive woman, but her expression was an unhappy and exasperated one. With her was her anxious husband, an equally handsome and trim man. Talia's mother was in the room as well, looking apprehensive.

Two years of progressively worsening headaches had brought Talia to me. An MRI had shown an aneurysm. Sitting across from them, I turned the computer screen around so they could see the small bump on a blood vessel in her brain. Thankfully, the bump didn't qualify as an aneurysm that was in danger of rupturing.

"The bulge on your vessel is not dangerous, and it is not causing your headaches," I told her. My news was obviously surprising to her.

We discussed her headaches and symptoms. Talia said that her two years of headaches had begun to worsen in the last six months. I asked if she had experienced any emotional traumas in that time. She paused to consider my question.

"My son Robbie died two years ago, and I don't think I'm over it yet," she replied. "I doubt that I will ever be the same again."

Lymphoma took Robbie's life when he was just 18 years old. As Talia told me this, her pain was visible.

"Do you have a faith or religion?" I asked.

She shrugged. "Christian, I guess, but I don't go to church."

"Did you stop going to church when your son died?" I asked.

"Yeah," she replied flatly, staring at the wall behind me.

I didn't want to offend her, knowing that she no longer expressed a faith. But I couldn't ignore this shell of a woman. For, in a place where there was beauty and there should have been joy, there was none. I couldn't leave her like this without trying to rescue her from that dark place.

"Whenever a child dies before a parent, it is a tremendous blow," I began. "There is often a great sense of injustice.

"I can't explain why Robbie died, but I can attest that God gave him grace to go through his trial two years ago."

She nodded. I paused, and then continued carefully.

"Watching Robbie suffer, you may have taken offense at God. It is very common to become angry and take up a grudge against God when those we love go through difficult times. But when we do that, we are in a dangerous and lonely place."

"You're right," she said, frowning. "Robbie seemed to have a peace about it, but I have a problem with it. I don't understand why God thought I could do this—that I could actually live without Robbie." A spark of anger flashed in her eyes.

I have seen unresolved anger turn into resentment and bitterness. And bitterness against anyone, including God, can cause illness. I believe we must release our resentment toward God through recognizing that he loves us and always has the best intentions for us—even if it doesn't appear true because of the pain we experience.

"I wonder if there are some things for which you are thankful, things that happened before and after Robbie died," I suggested.

She sat back in her chair and thought. Expressionless, she began to name a few things—her job, her daughter, her husband. I reminded her of her resources and education, and she lifted her eyebrows in recognition of these blessings. She smiled slightly and said that she was thankful for those things. As she continued to give thanks, her countenance began to change.

At this point, I sensed that she needed affirmation. I looked into her eyes.

"God is not angry with you," I said. "He is not punishing you. He is not disappointed with you."

I paused and then said quietly, "I know that he misses you."

Talia stared straight ahead, over my shoulder, unresponsive. However, out of the corner of my eye, I saw her husband nod.

"You have a sensitive heart and a sensitive spirit. You are still grieving the loss of your son," I continued. "And that's okay."

She nodded her head slowly in agreement.

"God's relationship with Robbie is between God and Robbie—just as God's relationship with you is just between the two of you. It may be hard for you to imagine, but God loves Robbie even more than you do," I said.

She blinked and tilted her head. I don't think she had ever considered God's love for Robbie as being greater than her own.

"Unfortunately, the *why* questions rarely get answered in this life. I encourage you to ask *what* or *how* questions instead," I prompted her.

"'What do you want me to know about you that will help me through this, God?' 'How do you want me to move forward?' 'What should I do with my feelings of despair?' Take time to listen for the answers. God wants to speak to you."

She nodded but did not smile. I wanted to connect Talia with her God—the only one who could breathe life into her joyless shell. I asked Talia if I could pray for her.

Quietly, she said, "Yes."

I stood at her side with my hand on her left shoulder. Her husband put his hand on her right shoulder. I asked God to bless her life with knowing how much he loved her, giving her clarity and purpose. I asked God to bless her with healing from her debilitating headaches. I blessed her marriage, sensing that it was at a breaking point because of her depression, and then I blessed her with good life choices and decisions.

Talia nodded slightly after the prayer, and her eyes appeared brighter than when she came in. As she left the exam room, she seemed tranquil. Her husband and her mother shook my hand warmly and thanked me.

A few months later, I received a letter from Talia. She told me she was healed from her physical pain, but that she was also healed from so much more.

"Thank you for looking beyond the surface and really seeing me," she wrote. "Since Robbie died, I had convinced myself never to relinquish my grip on my grief. I had confined him to a timeless loop of 'goneness,' a place where it is cold—like the emptiness between planets. This space was safe because it helped me avoid terror and truth.

"In the process, I locked up my heart and lost both myself and Robbie. You recognized the death in me, but also the life. Thank you for speaking life into my vortex of darkness. As you did, I was able to breathe my first breath since Robbie died. Since that hour in your office, I've had many conversations with God—conversations of sadness, anger, love, hope, and joy—and I have learned that he is still with me. I am experiencing transformation and healing. This is a new beginning for me."

My experience with Talia reminds me why I take the time to see my patients as individuals with unique life stories and to ask spiritual questions. This is particularly true when I have no physical explanation for their symptoms. In my exam room, God can begin to heal a broken heart and set a captive free.

Dr. David Levy is clinical professor of neurosurgery at the University of California, San Diego. He specializes in treating patients with brain aneurysms and diseases of the blood vessels of the brain. His articles have been published in a variety of medical journals. His book about praying with his patients, Gray Matter: A Neurosurgeon Discovers the Power of Prayer . . . One Patient at a Time, *written with Joel Kirkpatrick, was published by Tyndale House in February 2011. "A New Beginning" was written as "Beyond Physical Healing" with MaryAnn Nguyen-Kwok and adapted from* Today's Christian Doctor *(Spring 2011), a publication of the Christian Medical and Dental Associations.*

8

A Heart for Haiti

WILLIAM D. CRIBBS, DO

FAMILY PRACTICE

MARCO ISLAND, FLORIDA

There is no exercise better for the heart
than reaching down and lifting people up.

JOHN ANDREW HOLMES

Aimee's mother stood in front of me as I examined her little girl at the makeshift rural clinic in the Haitian parish of Lavaneau.

She had come a long way with her daughter to this tiny, mountainside church with gravel floors and no windows. Sheets had been thrown over wires and ropes to divide the church into exam cubicles.

I listened to Aimee's heart. There was no mistaking the murmur I heard.

"Did you know your daughter had this condition?" I asked her mother through a translator.

Yes, she did know something was wrong, the mother answered. When Aimee played, she would faint from the exertion, and she often missed school. But the family had nine children, all living in a one-room house, and no money to pay for medical treatment.

I thought for a minute.

"Would you permit Aimee to come to the United States with me to have her heart fixed?" I asked her.

What a question! As a parent myself, it was an awful thought. I can't imagine allowing my child to go off on such a journey with a stranger. Aimee was just nine years old. But if she didn't have the surgery, her survival in the harsh conditions of this desperately poor country was doubtful.

I arranged to meet Aimee, along with her mother and father, at the hotel where our medical team stayed each time we came to Haiti. Father Domond, the priest of the Haitian Catholic church that housed the clinic, came with them. Father Mike, from the Illinois church that sponsored our medical team, joined us.

"Now, Aimee," I said, "you understand that the government will not let your parents come with you. You would be traveling without them. But we would take good care of you."

Aimee said she understood, and Father Domond offered to accompany her—it didn't matter to him that Aimee's family was Baptist and that I attend a Presbyterian church.

"I'm doing this for God," he said simply. Her parents agreed, and it was settled.

Even so, I had no idea of how—or even if—I could do this.

To confirm my diagnosis, we wanted Aimee to have a few medical tests. I arranged for her and her mother to stay at Hospice St. Joseph's in Port-au-Prince, where I knew the nuns would take good care of them. The echocardiogram and electrocardiogram were done locally, and the results clearly showed an atrial septal defect, a hole in the wall between the atrial chambers of her heart.

But how would we pay for her surgery? The first estimate I got was $100,000 from a medical center well known for its cardiac care. Through some Rotary connections, though, we soon discovered that the Gift of Life program could offer the surgery at a pediatric hospital for just $5,000. Still, we needed to find a sponsor.

After our team returned to the States, I called a friend to say I had gotten back safely. This was a fellow who had been skeptical of my sudden desire at age 77 to start traveling to Haiti.

"If you do go, take a gun," he had warned me. Yet after I mentioned Aimee's need, he called me back.

"My wife and I will give you the money," he said. A generous neighbor volunteered to pay Aimee's way to the United States.

It took a while for Father Domond to arrange the paperwork for Aimee's trip and to have himself declared her legal guardian while she was here. Some months later, Aimee flew to Hollywood, Florida, where two couples from the medical team met her and checked her into Joe DiMaggio Children's Hospital. The surgery went well.

On the day following Aimee's surgery, my wife and I arrived at the hospital, eager to see how she was doing. As we walked into the room, we stopped for a moment to take in the scene.

Father Domond stood at Aimee's bedside, holding her hand. He was softly singing in Creole the old hymn, "How Great Thou Art."

> Then sings my soul, My Savior God to Thee;
> How great Thou art! How great Thou art!
> Then sings my soul, My Savior God to Thee;
> How great Thou art! How great Thou art!

"Come, Aimee, sing with me," he implored her gently, in his lilting English.

Tears started to roll from Aimee's eyes, and quietly she started to sing.

I will treasure this vision for the rest of my life—the two of them in that hospital room so far from home, singing of the power of God. To see God put this all together was the privilege of a lifetime.

Dr. William Cribbs retired after 40 years in family practice, first in Ohio, and later in Pennsylvania and New Jersey. In the 12 years of his retirement, he has volunteered at the Neighborhood Health Clinic in Naples, Florida, and has taken six medical mission trips to Haiti in association with Blessed Sacrament Catholic Church in Quincy, Illinois. He and his wife, Nancy, have five children and seven grandchildren.

9

DITCHING IN THE HUDSON

ANDREW JAMISON, MD

DERMATOLOGY

GREENVILLE, SOUTH CAROLINA

On January 15, 2009, US Airways Flight 1549 was forced to make an emergency landing in the Hudson River after a bird strike crippled its engines. Miraculously, all 155 passengers and crew members survived. Dr. Andrew Jamison was on that plane.

On January 15, 2009, I was in New York City for a residency interview. I had a ticket for a 9:30 P.M. US Airways flight from LaGuardia Airport to Charlotte, North Carolina. When the interview ended early, I got myself on standby for Flight 1549, leaving at 2:45 P.M. I was fortunate, I thought, to get a seat.

As with any other plane trip, I wasn't paying much attention at the start. I had been reading two books during the trip, *The Sovereignty of God* by Arthur W. Pink and *Prince Caspian* by C. S. Lewis. As we sat on the runway waiting for the plane to take off, I kept on reading. When the plane was cleared for takeoff at about 3:25 P.M., I wasn't listening as the flight attendant explained that in the unlikely event of a water landing, our life vests were under our seats.

The takeoff seemed to be going normally, when about a few min-utes into the flight there was a loud thud, and the plane lurched. My first thought was that this was just a little turbulence, but just to make sure, I glanced at the flight attendant. This has always been my gauge as to whether or not I should worry. She was visibly concerned.

I was in the very back of the plane, but somebody further forward said they saw the engine spark and start to smoke. I could smell smoke coming into the plane. That got my attention, and I put my book down. At the time, I thought just the right engine was affected, since that was the side of the plane I was sitting on.

With my limited knowledge of aircraft, I knew we only needed one engine to fly, which is what I told the woman sitting beside me.

"We can get all the way to Charlotte on one engine if we have to," I told her confidently.

Then it was quiet, too quiet, and I realized that both engines were out. The flight attendant was digging around the seat behind me, looking for a transponder or something, so it was clear that whatever was happening was not normal. It all happened very fast; I'd say that within thirty seconds I knew we were going down.

That knowledge seemed to hit everybody at the same moment, and we were all stunned. I tried to call my wife Jennifer to say good-bye, but my cell phone wouldn't work. Then I turned to the woman beside me, and perhaps from working in a context where you have to always ask permission to pray with somebody, I asked her if it was okay if I said a prayer. She looked at me like I was crazy, but she said, "Of course."

So the woman and I, along with the man who was sitting beside us, leaned in and bowed our heads. I don't remember word for word what I said, but since I was reading *The Sovereignty of God,* it was probably something like this:

"God, we know that you are sovereign, and that you are in control of planes, even planes without engines. We pray that your will be done. I ask for a peace that surpasses all understanding to descend upon all of us. And, God, I pray that if there is anyone listening who doesn't know you, that you would make it clear to them right now what your Son has done for us."

There wasn't much panic. Some passengers were saying "Hail Mary's," and you could hear some sobbing and crying, but no screaming or carrying on like you might expect.

About the time we finished our prayer, the captain came on over the speakers and said, "Brace for impact."

I am often asked what it was like when we hit the water. I honestly cannot give a good answer. At that time, I was expecting to get ripped to pieces. But what I remember most about the landing was feeling the almost immediate rush of extremely cold water at my feet. It started at my ankles, and by the time the plane came to rest, the water was up to my knees. All of a sudden a new fear crept into my mind: *I am going to drown! I can't get off the plane. I can't see the exits.*

Almost subconsciously, I reviewed my options for trying to save myself from drowning. I thought that maybe I could hold my breath long enough to swim to the back exit, or that maybe I could kick out a window—a ridiculous thought, in hindsight.

When I stood up, I could see that the nearest exit was behind me at the back of the plane. A passenger was struggling, unsuccessfully, in chest-high water to push it open. At the rate the water was rising, it seemed clear that we didn't have much time.

Suddenly, however, the water stopped rising. Passengers ahead of me were able to open other exits, and everyone began to leave the plane in an orderly fashion.

I was one of the last passengers off, and I exited through the left front door, using the emergency slide that doubles as a raft. With a great sense of relief and praise, I asked everyone in the raft if I could say another prayer, this one a prayer of thanksgiving. And I did.

After all the passengers and crew had gotten safely out of the plane, the captain, whose name we all know now—Captain Chesley B. "Sully" Sullenberger—and his co-captain, Jeffrey Skiles, got into the raft, and we cut ourselves free from the sinking plane. As we waited for the ferry boats to reach us, the pilots talked about how very few successful water ditchings there had ever been. As they talked, it really hit me: *This truly was an extraordinary event.*

When I finally did get to call Jennifer, she wondered if I was in my right mind. I had just survived a plane crash, and all I really wanted to say was: "God is great! God is great!"

I could say that in all honesty because, for me, the greatest miracle of that day wasn't the successful landing. After we had prayed and were going down, I experienced a peace that I truly can't explain. I fully expected to die within a few seconds, and yet it was okay. Even as we braced for impact, I was enveloped by a remarkable comfort and peace.

The Lord has continued to provide merciful psychological shielding for me. The night after the crash, I had one of the best nights of sleep I have ever had. To this day, I haven't had any nightmares or troubling dreams. And I still believe that reading *The Sovereignty of God* prepared me better for the crash than knowing where to find my life vest!

Dr. Andrew Jamison is in practice at GHS/Carolina Dermatology of Greenville, South Carolina. He and his wife, Jennifer Jamison, MD, a family physician, have two daughters.

"Ditching in the Hudson" was published as "In the Unlikely Event of a Water Landing" and adapted with permission from Today's Christian Doctor *(Winter 2009), a publication of the Christian Medical and Dental Associations. Dr. Jamison's story in the magazine was based in part on an interview conducted by David Stevens, MD, chief executive officer of the CMDA. Dr. Jamison expanded on his experience in a book titled* In the Unlikely Event of a Water Landing: Lessons from Landing in the Hudson River *(Healthy Life Press and CreateSpace, 2010), with a foreword by Dr. Stevens.*

10

GOD'S WAY OUT

ELAINE LEONG ENG, MD, DFAPA

PSYCHIATRY

QUEENS, NEW YORK

And we know that God causes everything to work together for the good
of those who love God and are called according to his purpose for them.

ROMANS 8:28

"Are you alright?"

I was on my way to a history class at Princeton University in the evening of a late fall day. It wasn't the usual location for the class, and I was struggling to find the path that led to the door of the building. My professor had noticed.

Embarrassed and confused, I said meekly, "I'm okay, Professor."

Then I followed him into the building by listening to the sound of his footsteps.

There were times at Princeton when I shied away from walking the dark campus at night for fear of falling into the lake or of getting lost. I assumed that I was experiencing night blindness of some sort. Because of my upbringing by Chinese parents, I thought the fault might be a carrot-poor diet, a common assumption in that culture. Or, given my heavy course load, it could be a lack of sleep.

At any rate, I thought it was something that could be fixed.

As I progressed through my medical training, I began to notice other sight deficiencies—"floaters" that obscured my vision, and even greater worsening of my night vision—but I always had an excuse. While I was doing my ob/gyn residency at Bellevue Hospital, I found myself bumping into furniture, especially the platforms we stood on to examine women in labor. My shins were perpetually marked with bruises. Still, I thought I might just be clumsy or sleep deprived. And, anyway, the lighting in labor rooms is low, I told myself.

As a resident trainee, my vision troubles didn't seem to affect my work adversely. Half the time in ob/gyn situations, such as in pelvic exams, you're going more by touch than by sight anyway. But I was also called on to teach interns and junior residents how to do deliveries and Caesarean sections, and I found myself unable to clearly see some of the things they were doing, such as suturing.

Perhaps I just need stronger glasses, I'd think to myself.

One day, I mentioned my vision to a colleague, who was concerned enough to suggest that I see his eye doctor. I was 29 years old at the time. I met with the doctor and had a thorough exam and consultation.

"Based on what I'm seeing," the ophthalmologist told me, "the changes in your vision are characteristic of retinitis pigmentosa."

Retinitis pigmentosa! Having been through medical school, I knew what RP was. It's a genetic eye disorder that leads to total and untreatable blindness. The doctor's face registered concern. He was sorry to have to deliver this news.

Imagine his surprise when I took the news calmly—not only calmly, but with thankfulness in my heart!

Five years earlier, I had married and quickly become the mother of a son and a daughter. Our son Brian came along just before I graduated medical school. Two years later, my daughter Genevieve arrived. In fact, the labor pains bringing her into the world began while I was on call at the hospital delivering other women's babies.

Yet my grueling schedule at the hospital often meant that I didn't see my children for days at a time. My long hours at the hospital, being on overnight call every third night, and the long commute home made it impossible to see Brian and Gen for more than a few hours every other night at most.

I was distraught by my divided loyalties between career and motherhood. I found that I could not be fully happy at home or at work. When I was home, I would worry about my patients. Yet when I was at the hospital, I longed to be with my babies. I was tortured by my inability to be the mom I wanted to be.

In my full life, there was little time for God, no room for leisure, and no time for my marriage. I wondered how my husband could put up with my all-consuming study and clinical rotation schedule. Life evolved into a long list of responsibilities. Medicine is a strict taskmaster.

God had made a way out for me.

Once I learned my diagnosis, I knew that I could not ethically practice in a surgical subspecialty. I resigned the next day.

Finally, I had the opportunity I craved to be a full-time mother to my babies! I could watch them grow while I still had some eyesight left. We lived in a large, sun-filled apartment where I held my children close, no longer forced to turn them over to someone else's care, their bereft cries stinging me as I turned my back on them yet again. We were happy singing songs, reading books, eating meals together. The kids zoomed around the apartment on their Smurf and Knight Rider bikes, their happy faces shining. These images and memories are permanently ingrained in my mind, as clear as a photo album.

Blindness—this so-called tragedy—brought good into my life. Don't misunderstand me. I would not have anyone think blindness is easy. It is not. I rely on family and friends, and I've used a cane. I have a guide dog, and my office is stuffed with eight pieces of technical equipment that help me read, write, and interact with the world. Blind people face many hardships and challenges. To say that coping with these difficulties has been pure joy would be a psychological denial of massive proportions.

Yet even at the moment of my diagnosis, there was a peace in my heart and a conviction in my spirit that all would work out well. I knew it was God's way of granting my prayer to be a full-time mom to my babies. God had prepared my heart to accept this news. I cannot explain this in human terms. To me, it was divine intervention—in simple terms, it was a miracle.

Dr. Elaine Leong Eng has had a private psychiatric practice in Queens, New York, for 20 years and is Clinical Assistant Professor of Psychiatry in the Department of Obstetrics and Gynecology at Weill-Cornell Medical College. She is a Distinguished Fellow in the American Psychiatric Association. Prior to her career in psychiatry, she had planned to be an ob/ gyn physician. She is trained in the Lay Ministry Program of Concordia College and has served on the board of directors of the Boro Pregnancy Counseling Center in Queens. She and her husband, Clifford, have two children, Brian and Genevieve. Portions of "God's Way Out" are adapted with permission from Dr. Eng's books, The Transforming Power of Story *(Healthy Life Press, 2010), coauthored with David B. Biebel, and* A Christian Approach to Overcoming Disability: A Doctor's Story *(The Haworth Pastoral Press, 2004).*

11

THE PORCH STEPS

BRENDA DRAPER, MD
COSMETIC PLASTIC SURGERY
ASHEVILLE, NORTH CAROLINA

He will wipe every tear from their eyes, and there will be no more death
or sorrow or crying or pain. All these things are gone forever.

REVELATION 21:4 NLT

I was in the third year of my general surgery training at a Level 1 trauma center in North Carolina. I was seeing a lot of gunshots, a lot of knife wounds, motorcycle accidents. The patients were mostly young kids, and many of them didn't survive.

The work was becoming overwhelming, and I was plagued with questions: *Why all the suffering? Does it never end? What happens to these kids after they die?* It felt as though I was just patching kids up so they could go out and get shot again. It wasn't what I had imagined I would be doing.

One night, the EMTs brought in a 19-year-old young man they found on a sidewalk, bleeding from gunshot wounds to his chest and abdomen. Jackson wasn't conscious, and he didn't have a pulse. As we wheeled him into the operating room, he never once opened his eyes.

We prepared for the surgery, quickly putting up a drape to shield our work. I didn't have a lot of hope for his survival. Even if he did survive, I wondered what his long-term chances would be.

We began the surgery and sometime into it removed Jackson's spleen, which was damaged beyond repair. Suddenly, we were surprised to get a pulse and a blood pressure reading. We were startled—it was so unlikely. We continued with the surgery.

After we finished, I washed up while Jackson was wheeled into the recovery room and his breathing tube removed. I came in to check on him, still gowned for surgery.

As I took off my hat and mask, Jackson opened his eyes and said softly, "Hey, Doc."

I was shocked. Patients don't generally come out of anesthesia so quickly—it just doesn't happen that way. Jackson was groggy, but alert.

"How are you doing?" I asked him.

"I remember you," Jackson answered. "You were in there."

In where? The operating room? I thought. *How could he know that? He never opened his eyes.* I shrugged it off, thinking the anesthesia was still affecting him.

"You were the one who started," Jackson went on, "and then a tall guy in a cap came in."

Jackson was right—I had started the surgery. As I worked, the chief resident came into the operating room. This doctor always wore a cap, and his thick, curly hair stuck out around it.

One by one, Jackson described everyone who had been in the operating room—the anesthesiologist, the scrub nurse, the other nurses.

"There was another person there. He was short, and he had to stand on something," Jackson continued.

A medical student had observed the surgery, and he had stood on a stepstool.

I started to feel a little shaky. *Wasn't that drape up? How could he possibly have seen all this?* He never opened his eyes, as far as we knew.

A sudden fear gripped my heart. Had we not given him enough anesthesia? Had he been awake while we operated?

"Did we hurt you?" I asked Jackson.

"No," Jackson replied. "No, you guys did a great job. I was watching you. There was some bleeding, and then you took something out, something big and red."

The human spleen is a large, purplish-red organ.

"Where were you?" I asked Jackson.

"I'm not sure," he answered, "but I was in the room. My mom was there with me. She was talking to me. She said, 'Son, you need to get your life together.'

"She told me, 'You need to take care of your grandmother. Your life is causing her a lot of stress and anguish. You need to get out of the gang.'"

"Is your mother alive?" I asked Jackson.

"No, she's been dead for five years," he said.

Alive or dead, Jackson's mother apparently was a very practical woman, because she had some further instructions for her son.

"Your grandmother has hip trouble. You have to fix her porch steps before she falls down. The third step from the top is bad," Jackson remembers his mother saying.

"Then, my mother started drifting away," Jackson said. "She was saying, 'You can't go with me. You're not ready for this place.' And then they rolled me in here and took that thing out of my mouth."

My mind was reeling. Oddly enough, it wasn't the reference to an otherworldly place that got my attention. It was the specific instructions regarding the porch steps. Jackson confirmed that he lived with his grandmother, and that her house had a porch with steps.

Jackson's recovery went well, and in time he was released from the hospital. I saw him some time later, when he came in for a checkup at the residency clinic. He talked a little more about his experience in the operating room.

He told me that he, too, had been taken aback by the instructions regarding the porch steps.

"When I went back to live with my grandma, I looked at the steps and sure enough, the third step down was rotted and about to cave in, and the railing was coming loose," he said. His grandmother could have had a terrible accident. Jackson fixed the steps.

"I still don't know where I was during the operation," he said. "But I felt like I was floating, like I was riding on a gentle wave."

Transformed by his experience, Jackson left the gang and began working as a groundskeeper for a church. He asked me whether I could do anything about the tattoos on his arm identifying him as a member of his former gang.

Later, Jackson returned to the clinic with four of his buddies from the gang. Using laser treatments, I removed all of their tattoos. Jackson went on to start a landscaping business with his friends, and he began speaking to groups of young people, warning them of the dangers of gang life.

Twenty years later, I still get chills when I think about Jackson. I don't know for sure what happened, but I think now that maybe all of what Jackson experienced took place while he had no pulse, and that his vision of his mother faded away as his pulse and blood pressure returned.

Whatever happened in that operating room, it removed a lot of my doubts. Jackson never said the word *heaven*, but he described to me a place of peace. I thought of all my young patients, my last images of them in their agony, and now I imagined them in this other place, free at last from their pain. Through Jackson, I was given the incredible gift of belief.

Dr. Brenda Draper has been in practice since 1982 and is a cosmetic plastic surgeon at Asheville Aesthetic Plastic Surgery in Asheville, North Carolina. She performs elective surgical and nonsurgical procedures, including breast reconstruction after cancer surgery. She has two children, Cole and Joshua.

12

THE OPEN BLINDS

MARK GRUBB, MD

PEDIATRIC MEDICINE

PUYALLUP, WASHINGTON

Some years ago, when our clinic was smaller than it is today, I was on call for our three doctors one Saturday night. I was teaching a teen-aged friend how to drive at the time, and I was in a car with him when my cell phone went off. It was the hospital calling.

"It's an emergency!" the caller said. "You need to get to the delivery room right away."

As it happened, we were just driving past the hospital when the call came in. My young friend pulled over and let me out. I ran for the delivery room.

When I got there, I found a familiar family. The wife was expecting twins and had gotten excellent care from an obstetrician I knew well. But now, something was wrong.

As the woman's labor had progressed, the doctor discovered a terrible complication, a rare condition called vasa previa. When this happens, blood vessels from the placenta or umbilical cord leading to the baby have grown over the cervical opening beneath it. As the baby is born, the blood vessels tear or become pinched, and the baby doesn't get enough blood. In fact, blood from the baby drains out when it is squeezed in the process of birth.

To my knowledge, vasa previa was always a fatal event for the baby.

My obstetrician friend moved faster than any doctor I've ever seen. He prepped the woman and performed a C-section in minutes flat. In an unusual bit of foresight, he called for units of blood for the unfortunate baby.

The baby was immediately ushered into the nursery. I took a quick glance and didn't like what I saw. It was a boy, and he was completely white, as white as a sheet. He had no heart rate and no pulse. Worse, he had no blood whatsoever. This was not only a dead child, but a completely bloodless baby.

I established a line to the baby's belly button and began to perform cardiopulmonary resuscitation. But CPR isn't any good unless a person has blood, so we began to introduce blood into the baby's vessels. We had no time to calculate how much the baby should get, so we just kept going until I thought the amount was right.

We intubated him in order to facilitate breathing, but 15 minutes passed and still the baby had no heart rate. If you can't get any vital signs within 10 or 15 minutes, a person most often suffers such severe neurological damage that you don't do anyone any favors by continuing. I kept this in mind as we tried to revive the baby.

At 16 minutes, I decided it was time to call an end to the resuscitation effort.

Just then, though, I happened to glance up at the nursery window. Usually, the blinds on the windows are closed, but in the teeth of the emergency, we hadn't bothered to see to this. The blinds were open. Outside, in the waiting area, the extended family was gathered.

At just the moment I looked up, a family member said, "Let's pray." Everyone went down on their knees.

As the family began to implore God for help, I decided it wasn't time to give up. I called for continued efforts, and we watched as the clock ticked past 17 minutes. Still nothing.

But at 18 minutes, I saw a little blip on the screen.

"Okay," I said to everyone. "Let's keep going."

Then I saw another blip, and another. The baby's heart started to beat, and he began to turn pink.

Although this was a hopeful sign, I fully expected to see seizures at any moment. This would have been the normal outcome. We kept up our efforts, even as I anticipated the worst. Yet something in me said that this was not a normal case.

Just then, we heard small gasping sounds.

"Let's pull the breathing tube and see what happens," I suggested.

When we removed the tube, the baby started breathing on his own. His blood pressure rose and he began pinking up even more. No sign of seizures.

"Let's stop our support efforts altogether," I said, gaining confidence.

We stopped, waited, and then the baby began coughing and moving around a little. Still no sign of seizures. Incredibly, at 20 minutes, the baby's health and physical condition tests were perfectly fine.

I stayed with the baby for an hour. There was no need to even transfer him to an intensive care unit. He and his twin were both healthy. I saw the family again when the child was two years old, and he had met all the expected milestones. I have done some research, and I can't find any other occurrence of vasa previa in which a baby who needed a complete blood transfusion lived and developed normally.

But on that day, there was no fanfare. The parents knew that tragedy had been very close, but their thanks weren't necessary. We had all just done our jobs. It was God who did something really special, something really wild, that day. It was a miracle, something completely outside of medicine, and we all knew it. I feel privileged to have been a part of it.

Dr. Mark Grubb is a pediatrician at Woodcreek Healthcare in Puyallup, Washington. He has practiced medicine since 1985. Dr. Grubb has patented a medical device that has been successfully used to treat earaches without the use of antibiotics or tubes. He and his wife, family practitioner Nancy Grubb, MD, have two daughters, Laura and Elizabeth.

13

A Chance Encounter

MICHAEL HUNT, MD

PEDIATRIC OPHTHALMOLOGY

FORT WORTH, TEXAS

Be faithful in small things because it is in them that your faith lies.

MOTHER TERESA

Our team was waiting for the overnight train to Hanoi after spending a week in the rural province of Lao Cai in northern Vietnam.

This was the first time I had gone with a team from our church—a church smack in the middle of the Bible belt of America!—to work in this Communist country. I was part of a team of six people. We were exploring what kind of work we might be able to do here on a continuing basis. Some of the team taught health and hygiene issues—even a plumber had even come along with us to help with a water filtration project.

In Hanoi, I gave lectures on eye care, such as cataract surgery and pediatric eye care, to specialists at the Vietnamese National Institute of Ophthalmology. In Lao Cai, a primitive area that borders China, I gave similar talks at a provincial hospital.

But we spent most of our time screening people to see if we could correct their vision with glasses. We screened adults at the hotel where we were staying. We screened children at schools and orphanages. We worked with a local optical shop to make glasses for those who needed them. We also brought glasses with us that had been donated by folks back home.

After we had determined what each person needed, we first tried to match them up with glasses having the closest prescription we could manage. Sometimes, it wasn't quite the right prescription; maybe the right lens was correct, but the left one wasn't, or maybe both lenses were slightly off. But in any case, something was better than nothing. We just did the best we could.

Whatever glasses we gave out, even if it wasn't exactly the right prescription, they made a big difference for the recipient. One elderly gentleman living at the orphanage because he had no family was so pleased with his glasses that he walked around the grounds, smiling and laughing, and showing them off to everyone he came across.

To be honest, when I was deciding whether or not to go on this trip, I was worried about the loss of income my absence would impose on our new clinic in the States. But when I saw what a difference a simple pair of glasses made—a pair that might cost only twenty-five dollars in U.S. currency but was still unaffordable to most people in Vietnam—any thought of lost income was swallowed up in the sheer joy on our patients' faces.

But now our trip was coming to an end, and it was time to return to Hanoi, and then head back to the States. The train station at Lao Cai City is a busy place, so we were glad to have a guide from our church, who had many trips under his belt, to get us to the right train.

While we waited for our train, our guide took us into a small restaurant at the station for a bite to eat. He apparently had come into the restaurant before, as he greeted the waitress warmly and talked companionably with her. When he told her what our group was doing in Lao Cai, she became very excited.

Of course, we couldn't understand what the waitress was saying, but she pointed to an elderly Vietnamese woman sitting alone in a corner at the back of the restaurant. Our guide said the woman was the waitress's mother.

"She wants to know if you can do anything to help her. She can't see well," our guide said.

I accompanied the waitress over to her mother's table and got out my equipment, a battery-operated light, and lenses for determining prescriptions. I examined the old woman's eyes and found that she needed lenses for distance viewing and reading glasses for seeing up close.

We had given away all our reading glasses, but I rummaged through our boxes of donated glasses to see how close we could come to what she needed. I pulled out a pair of bifocals for her to try on.

It was her prescription exactly!

The woman's daughter brought over a menu for her mother to read. When she found she could read the print, she smiled a wide smile. Even her bearing changed, as her corrected vision restored a confidence and joy she had lost as her sight had deteriorated and her world shrank.

Despite the language barrier, we knew how much these glasses meant to this woman. She and her daughter were effusive in their thanks. We went on our way marveling at the providential hand of God.

For me, this chance encounter in a Vietnam train station confirmed my belief that God often has plans that we know nothing about in advance. It hasn't got anything to do with our *ability*—it's all about our *availability*.

Dr. Michael Hunt is an ophthalmologist whose practice, Pediatric Eye Specialists, is in Fort Worth, Texas. He and the practice's other physicians have founded Child Vision Center, a nonprofit research and diagnostic center that provides care locally, as well as training for doctors from around the world who care for pediatric eye patients in their home countries. Dr. Hunt has taken five mission trips to North Vietnam with his church, Northwood Church, and the Vietnamese organization Global Ventures, Inc. He and his wife, Jennifer, have three children, Meghan, Griffin, and Nathan.

14

A WOUNDED MARINE

WILLIAM LASCHEID, MD

FORMER U.S. NAVY OFFICER

DERMATOLOGY

NAPLES, FLORIDA

Honor. Courage. Commitment.

U.S. MARINE CORPS CORE VALUES

The year 1951 was a whirlwind for me. In July, I finished up my internship, and in August, being in the Navy Reserve, I received orders to go to Camp Lejeune for basic training with the Marines. Six weeks later, I shipped out to Korea.

I arrived by plane in Korea and was put immediately into a jeep and driven directly to the front lines. It all happened so quickly, I was still in my dress uniform. I landed in what was known as "The Punchbowl," a deep circular valley in the mountains of Korea, attached to the 1st Battalion, 1st Marine Division.

Two days later, we came under an enemy mortar attack. The shelling was intense and a Marine in the bunker next to mine soon got hit. I needed to get over there to tend to his wounds.

I made my way to his bunker amid the enemy fire all around me. I tended to his wounds, which needed immediate attention. Four of us got him onto a stretcher and over to a waiting helicopter that had landed behind a nearby hill.

After we saw the Marine off safely, I returned to my bunker and to the needs of other Marines. Shortly afterward, I was transferred to an "E" Medical Unit, which is similar to a Mobile Army Surgical Hospital, or MASH, unit. I served there behind the front lines for almost a year. I was so young, and the Good Lord surely watched out for me. I was honorably discharged from the service in December 1953 and returned home to civilian life.

Fast forward 24 years to 1977. I had a practice in Pittsburgh, Pennsylvania. I arrived home late one winter night just as the telephone was ringing. My wife picked up the phone, and the caller asked if this was the home of Dr. Lascheid. She replied that it was, just assuming it was a patient. She handed the phone over to me as I walked in the door.

The caller identified himself as a Marine who had been wounded in Korea.

"Did you serve in Korea?" the caller asked. I said that I had. He asked whether I'd served with the 1st Battalion, 1st Marine Division, and I replied that I had.

The caller then identified himself as the Marine who had been wounded in that bunker!

In words broken with emotion, the former Marine said that while I was running alongside the gurney tending to his wounds, he tried to focus on the name on my uniform. He was slipping in and out of consciousness, yet he wanted to memorize the name of the young doctor tending to him. He noted that it was an unusual name and spelling—Lascheid.

After he returned home and recovered, he built a career as a sales-man and traveled extensively. Through the years, as he went from city to city, he'd pore through phone books, looking for a Dr. Lascheid. (This was in the era before the Internet could make a search like this so effortless.) He had done the same on his current trip to Pittsburgh.

After telling me his story, the caller concluded abruptly.

"Thank you for saving my life!" he blurted out. "I've been looking for you all these years to say thank you."

With that, he hung up. I didn't get the chance to say anything in return. The Marine's mission was apparently accomplished.

My wife and I were both speechless at the thought of this man's dogged determination. He'd spent more than a quarter of a century on his task, and finally he'd found his man. With no means of con-tacting him and inviting him to our home, which we surely would have done, she and I celebrated together that night. In awe, we raised our glasses to him and toasted yet another Marine of honor.

Dr. William Lascheid (1926–2014) served in the U.S. Navy from 1943 to 1955 in both World War II and in Korea, holding the rank of Lieutenant Junior Grade. He retired after 40 years from his dermatology practice in 1998. Two months later, he and his wife, Nancy, a registered nurse, founded the Neighborhood Health Clinic in Naples, Florida, to serve patients with few resources and no medical insurance. The clinic is staffed by hundreds of volunteer doctors, nurses, case workers, and other health care providers. The couple have five children, eleven grandchildren, and three great-grandchildren.

15

Only the Best in Post-Op Care

Sidney Barnes III, MD, FACS

General Surgery

Berlin, Maryland

As a resident, one of my rotations was caring for post-op patients in the intensive care unit of a hospital in Philadelphia.

The layout of the ICU was circular, with the nurses' station in the center of the wheel. From a patient's room, you could look across the nurses' station into another patient's room.

One time, we were caring for a trauma patient, a guy who had been stabbed in the chest multiple times. His lungs had collapsed, and he'd passed out while driving and crashed his car.

This patient was a bad guy, a really bad guy. He was a drug dealer, and his assault was part of a drug deal gone wrong. He was high on cocaine when he crashed his car, and they found drugs on board when they searched the car.

Despite his injuries, he wasn't all that bad off. All we needed to do was insert two small tubes, reinflate his lungs, and stitch him up. Still, because one of the side effects of cocaine use is heart arrhythmia, we needed to keep an eye on him. But he remained in the ICU, because there weren't any beds available in the cardiac unit.

This fellow was a miserable human being. As a patient, he treated everybody poorly, arguing and shouting obscenities at us. We had to put up with him for days on end, and it was wearing everyone down—doctors, nurses, aides, everyone.

One day while I was in the drug dealer's room, he and a doctor got into an argument. You could hear it all over the ICU. It went on for some time, and then the doctor shouted—and I'll give you the family-friendly version—"I told you to shut up! Just shut up!"

At that very moment, the patient went limp, and his eyes rolled back in his head. He went into what we call V Tach, or ventricular tachycardia, an irregular heart beat. If V Tach continues, the heart stops pumping and the patient's blood pressure drops. Unless the heart returns to normal function, the person will die.

We needed to restart the guy's heart, so I gave him a precordial thump. To do this, you make a fist with your hand and punch the center of the chest hard. All I could think was, *I just punched this guy in the chest—and he's going to kill me!* It did the trick, though, and the guy's heart started again.

Well, across the nurses' station, a patient, a frail elderly gentleman, was apparently watching the commotion from his room. He immediately hit the nurse call button. When the nurse hustled in to check on him, he was struggling to sit up and get dressed.

"I've got to get out of this hospital," he said to her, desperation in his voice. "One doctor just shouted at that patient to shut up, and then the other doctor beat him up!"

Dr. Sidney Barnes III practices general surgery at Atlantic General Hospital in Berlin, Maryland. He is a Fellow in the American College of Surgeons. He also provides medical support at Your Doc's In Urgent Care Center in Salisbury, Maryland, teaches surgery at the University of Maryland Eastern Shore, and is a surgical preceptor for its Physicians Assistant Department. He and his wife, Karen, have five children, Jennifer, Brian, Sean, Timothy, and Dan.

16

WHAT THE DOCTORS SAW

ROBERT PAEGLOW, MD

FAMILY MEDICINE

ALBANY, NEW YORK

As the heavens are higher than the earth,

so are my ways higher than your ways

and my thoughts than your thoughts.

ISAIAH 55:9

I have run a clinic in the poorest neighborhood of Albany, New York, for ten years. I've seen a lot of miracles in that time, and there are probably even more that I'll never even know about. But there is one instance that stands out above all the others, the most dramatic evidence of God's working that I have ever seen.

A few years ago, a young man just 24 years old came to me with a shoulder problem. I knew Luke and his family well—he and my daughter had grown up together in our church's youth group. He was handsome, all-American, in the prime of his life. He was an athletic man who regularly played in adult softball and basketball leagues. But now he was suffering from shoulder pain and a reduced range of motion.

I thought he most likely was suffering from frozen shoulder or ten-
donitis, which are common enough maladies among athletes. I sent
him to physical therapy, a course of action that generally speeds the
healing process in these situations.

A few weeks later, though, Luke came back to the clinic for a second
exam. The physical therapy hadn't helped. In fact, his pain was getting worse and his range of motion was even more compromised. This
struck me as odd in an otherwise young and healthy person.

I arranged for Luke to have an MRI at Albany Medical Center a few
days later. That same day, the radiologist called me.

"I've seen the film, Bob, and it's one of the worst cases of cancer
I've ever seen," she said.

The cancer had eaten into Luke's shoulder blade and humerus, the
upper bone of his arm. It was an aggressive cancer that needed immediate treatment.

I hung up the phone and leaned against the nurse's station. I just
began to cry. I felt so bad for this wonderful young man and his wife.

The next morning, I called Luke and his wife, Monica, into the
clinic. How do you tell a 24-year-old that his future is at risk? That
he might lose his arm—or even his life? I prayed to God for wisdom
and grace.

I ushered them into an exam room and sat down with them, the
radiologist's report in my hands. As gently as I could, I told them
about the cancer.

"We need to move on this right now," I said. "We can't afford to wait."

Of course, the news hit this young couple hard. When a doctor tells you
that you have cancer, it's like getting hit over the head. You're stunned, confused, hurt. The world stops. Luke and Monica cried as I broke the news.

No matter what news I have for my patients, I always try to offer comfort and hope—not false hope but *some* hope. I like to pray with all my patients. So that's what I did now.

"You've heard what the doctors have to say," I told them. "But we know that God has the final say, so let's pray."

I prayed for healing for Luke and that God would be glorified in his life. Before Luke and his wife had even arrived at the clinic, I had arranged for him to be seen that day by a friend of mine, an orthopedic surgeon.

My surgeon friend called me that same night.

"Bob, this is one of the worst cancers I've ever seen," he said. "It goes beyond what we can handle here. I'm going to refer Luke to a specialist in New York."

While I handled the health insurance forms and approvals, Luke and his wife went to the city to be seen by Dr. Steele at the special surgery hospital. Of course, Dr. Steele saw the cancer as well—lymphoma, a type of cancer involving cells of the immune system. Again, the diagnosis was a very advanced case.

"Luke's life is at risk," he said bluntly. He scheduled a biopsy for the next day.

The biopsy went off as planned, and the samples were taken immediately from the operating room to the lab to be analyzed. Yet again, I got a phone call.

"Doctor, I'm confused," said Dr. Steele. "I was 100 percent certain of Luke's lymphoma. I've seen hundreds of cases, so I know what it looks like."

"We've just analyzed the samples," he continued. "There is no cancer there. The cells have been burned out. I don't know what to tell you."

Wow! I thought. *That's great!*

But, to be honest, I was also aware that nothing but cancer eats into bone, so what else could it be? Had we missed something? I wanted to be sure, so I sent Luke back to Albany for a PET scan. Positron emission tomography allows doctors to look at cross-sectional images of organs and tissues at a cellular level. Cancer on a PET scan is obvious—the affected areas light right up.

After the scan, I got a call from the radiologist. This time it wasn't good news.

"We've seen what we think is cancer in the lymph nodes of the armpit," she said.

The news made me cringe. Cancer in the lymph nodes is bad news. I called in a general surgeon to do a lymph node biopsy.

At the medical center, the surgeon was accompanied into the OR by a medical student who had worked with me since Luke's first exam. They performed the lymph node surgery, as well as a few other procedures. Again I received a call, this time from the medical student.

"Dr. Bob, you're never going to believe this," she said. "We've just had the results of Luke's biopsy and tests. There is no cancer there."

With that news, there was great rejoicing! Where once there had been cancer—medically documented many times over—now there was no sign of it. I immediately got on the phone with Dr. Steele.

"What do you think of that?" I asked him.

"I think that's a miracle," he replied.

"Yep, I agree," I said.

Luke has been married for six years now, and he and his wife have two children. He has returned to his athletic pursuits. There is no sign of cancer in his body. Luke himself said he knew by the way he felt that he had been healed, even before we told him. I don't know why we were allowed this glimpse of God's glory. I pray for many patients who are not healed. I wonder why that is, but only God knows his plans. I only know that miracles do happen.

Dr. Robert Paeglow came to medicine late in life, beginning his training in his late 30s. He led mission trips to Mozambique and other African countries, experiences that cemented his resolve to make life better for the poor. He operates Koinonia Primary Care clinic in the West Hills neighborhood of Albany, New York, where he draws no salary, and he teaches at Albany Medical College. His wife, Liliane, is a nurse at the clinic. She and Bob have four adult children, Robert Jr., Rebecca, Corrie, and Amanda.

17

A Vision of Hell

PAUL K. CARLTON JR., MD

LT. GEN., USAF (RET.)

DIRECTOR, OFFICE OF INNOVATIONS

AND PREPAREDNESS

TEXAS A&M UNIVERSITY SYSTEM

HEALTH SCIENCE CENTER

COLLEGE STATION, TEXAS

A hero is no braver than an ordinary man,
but he is braver five minutes longer.

RALPH WALDO EMERSON

On September 11, 2001, I was in a senior staff meeting at the Pentagon. In a meeting like this, with the Chief of Staff and other high-ranking officers, you would never interrupt the proceedings. But on this day, there was a knock on the door and an Air Force officer entered. He turned on a television and showed us video of the airplanes hitting the Twin Towers.

At that moment, it was apparent to me that we were at war.

We were all directed to go to our battle stations. I went up to the Vice Chief's office to assess the situation in New York. He took a phone call, and while he was on the phone, the building shook, and it quickly filled with smoke. The third plane of the 9/11 terrorist attacks had struck.

Immediately, I headed for the Pentagon clinic to take a team into the center courtyard of the Pentagon. About 40 people from the clinic followed me and began forming triage teams. I was a three-star general at the time and the senior medical officer on the scene, but on this day, rank didn't mean anything. I reported to the fire chief, telling him we were ready to receive casualties.

Just then, a technical sergeant stepped out of the building and said, "Follow me!" I formed a litter team with the four people closest to me, and we headed into a corridor of the building in search of casualties.

The six of us headed down the corridor, but we were turned back by smoke and fire. We headed out into an alley between two corridors and came to the site of the crash. The landing gear of the plane had punched through the two outer rings of the building, bounced against the third, and come to rest in the alley where we stood.

Some of my colleagues said they had heard screams coming from inside the building as recently as five minutes earlier. We knew we needed to provide a lifeline for any survivors in the building. Our team had no choice but to go through the hole made by the plane.

We formed a line to pass debris and bodies out of the building. To begin with, I was outside the building, but when a man in front of me went down, I was next in line to go in. I turned to the Navy SEAL behind me and said, "You're in charge." Choosing that man, dressed unassumingly in shorts and a tank top but with the bearing of a military man, was the best decision I made that day.

Going through the hole was like passing into hell. We crawled over and through the wall of debris. There was fire on all sides and a jet of fire towering above me. It was like a blow torch over my head. The heat of the fire was melting the building, and hot, dripping metal seared our skin. Electricity arced from melting power lines, shocking us if we stood up. I didn't know it then, but at one point my clothes caught on fire. The man behind me started whopping on my back to put it out, but it didn't even register with me.

As we moved forward, we seemed to be entering a mangled wire cage. I realized it was a SCIF—a secure compartmented information facility—a type of room inside the Pentagon enmeshed in a wire cage to provide an added layer of security for top secret information.

Assaulted by the black, acrid smoke, we could barely see or breathe. You couldn't lift your head more than 18 inches off the ground without encountering the choking smoke. I made my way back out and shouted to several people to take off their T-shirts and soak them in water. I gathered up the wet shirts, went back into the building, and passed them out to the others. Having the cool water-soaked shirts over our mouths and noses was the only thing that allowed us to keep going. Those shirts gave us two or three more minutes to effect our rescues.

Three of us, two Navy men and I, managed to extract two women who were trapped in the SCIF. One woman screamed when she saw me—I must have looked like the devil himself. We passed them out of the building, and then we came to a man who was pinned under a table. His legs were immobilized, and a bookcase and chunks of ceiling had fallen on his head. There were three waterfalls of fire over his head and on either side of him.

But despite the smoke, I could see the man's face as clear as day. His eyes were closed. I needed to know whether he was alive or whether to move on, so I hit him in the face with a wet T-shirt. At the impact, he shook his head, so I knew he was alive.

Even as I did this, the roof over our heads was threatening to collapse. The Navy SEAL whom I'd left in charge outside came in behind us and quickly realized that the building was collapsing. He reached up and single-handedly held up the wire cage as pieces of concrete and steel crashed down on it. But the wire cage couldn't withstand much more weight and the heat was beginning to make the cage untouchable. It wouldn't be long before the ceiling caved in.

My colleague, a Navy physician, couldn't lift the table to free the man, so he got on his back, put his feet on the underside of the table, and did a leg press. This gave me enough room to pull the man out from under the table. I wedged a fire extinguisher under the table so that my colleague could get himself up off the floor without being crushed. Together we managed to pass the man out to safety.

"You need to get out of the building now!" the SEAL shouted. We wanted to go deeper, to hunt for more survivors, but the stridency of his tone struck me. He was in charge, and I needed to obey.

As we moved toward the hole we had entered through, the building suddenly collapsed. With the whoosh of a tremendous air wave, I was blown out of the building, along with the two other rescuers. We landed in a six-inch-deep puddle of water. From start to finish, the building had lasted only 19 minutes. Our rescues were accomplished in less than five minutes.

After the attack, I couldn't sleep at night for some time. I'd seen a vision of hell. You just don't understand the primal fear of fire until you've experienced it. To go into it is against every instinct you have. But what really kept me awake was that I did not know for several weeks what had happened to my team that day. I thank God they all came out alive.

At the Pentagon that day, 184 people died on the ground and in the plane. Ours were the last three rescues before the collapse of the building. I thank God that the number of casualties wasn't 187. It is our privilege as Christians to treasure every life.

Even as we mourned the 184 people who died, we realized that the day's tragedy could have been far worse than it was. In God's providence, some months earlier we had decided to conduct a training exercise. We were standing in a stairwell at the Pentagon one day in May when a plane from Ronald Reagan National Airport passed overhead.

"Let's do an airplane-hits-the-Pentagon exercise," a colleague suggested, not even imagining a terrorist scenario.

We planned and carried out the exercise and, based on the results of the exercise, set the "get well date" for September 1, the day on which all deficiencies identified in the exercise had to be put right. Because of the exercise, we had better protective clothing and equipment on hand, and we had drawn up evacuation plans. We had reinforced the sprinkler system—the system that I believe created the pool of water into which I was ejected.

But, in my mind, the real hero that day was the Navy SEAL. Not only did he save our lives, but he saved many other lives as well. He piled garbage cans on top of each other so he could reach windows, break them, and get people out. He saved the lives of four or five people who jumped from the burning building. I saw him catch two women who jumped—one he just caught in his arms, and it knocked him on his rear end. When he saw the second woman coming, he turned turtle, like he was in a football tackle, and he hit her at a calculated moment, so she came down horizontally instead of vertically, which saved both her life and his. He sustained facial injuries when the impact of her body ground his face into the pavement.

When I think back over it, I am certain I might have been dead ten times that day, if it weren't for God's protection. My staff, in fact, thought that I was dead, because I did not show up at an agreed-upon meeting point. After the attack, they moved to my house at Bolling Air Force Base and began conducting operations from my bedroom. Thankfully, they did not say anything of what they suspected to my wife. When I finally did get home, I walked into the bedroom wanting to shower and change, and there they all were, looking at me like they were seeing a ghost.

As a Christian I don't believe in coincidences, and I don't believe there were any that day. Through many circumstances, God provided me with a way out. While I know death is not a defeat, I believe God brought me back out into his light that day.

Dr. Paul K. Carlton Jr., Lt. Gen., USAF (Retired), served as Air Force Surgeon General from 1999 to 2002. As Surgeon General, he was functional manager of the U.S. Air Force Medical Service. His vision for medical care in the combat zone has led to the nation's current best survival rate in the history of warfare. To read about the Pentagon attack in more depth, see Ken Ringle's Smithsonian *article "Uncommon Valor" (September 2002) and the book* Firefight: Inside the Battle to Save the Pentagon on 9/11 *by Patrick Creed and Rick Newman (Ballantine Books, 2008). Dr. Carlton and his wife, Jan, have four grown children.*

18

In Her Heart

Jacob DeLaRosa, MD

Cardiothoracic Surgery

Pocatello, Idaho

Atiya went off to college with all the hopes and dreams of a young woman her age. But early in her freshman year, she began to feel unwell. Her symptoms were flu-like—headache, dizziness, a temperature—so she went to see the university's doctor. He prescribed antibiotics for her.

Even so, Atiya became sicker. Eventually, she was unable to continue her studies, and she flew home so her parents could care for her. By the time I saw Atiya, she had come into the emergency room and been admitted to the hospital. Regardless of the good care she was getting, her condition worsened, and she was transferred to the intensive care unit.

In the ICU, she quickly began to fail. She was septic, which means that a massive infection was ravaging her body. She was on intravenous antibiotics, and we put her on a breathing tube, yet still she weakened. Her organs were shutting down. I ordered an echocardiogram of her heart.

When the tests came back, I could see clearly what was happening. She had endocarditis, which is an inflammation of the inner lining of the heart due to infection. Bacteria and clots of blood—a substance we call vegetation—were pumping into her body through the bloodstream, coursing through all of her organs and her brain. She was having strokes as the vegetations were reaching her brain.

Atiya's family had been told the horrifying news that a parent hopes never to hear: *Your child may not live through this.* At this point, Atiya had a very low chance of survival, and even if she did survive, major neurological damage was almost certain.

I could perform surgery on Atiya's heart, but the conditions were not favorable. Usually, surgery is not an option for at least three weeks after vegetations have embolized to the brain. But we didn't have three weeks. Atiya was on supportive care, and she was dying.

I presented the situation to Atiya's parents.

"We can go ahead with the surgery, but if we do, there is only a 5 to 10 percent chance that Atiya will survive," I told them. "If she does survive, the chances of her coming through without suffering a severe, debilitating stroke are less than 1 percent."

After conferring, Atiya's parents asked me to go ahead with the surgery.

"Atiya's life is in God's hands through yours," they told me with quiet confidence.

Although our training as doctors enables us to dissociate from the emotions of heart-wrenching situations, I was deeply touched, and I struggled to switch off the empathy rising in my own heart. Atiya was so young and so pretty. *That could be my child. That could be me grieving,* I thought.

Not only that, but the entire time Atiya was at the hospital, prayer groups of forty and fifty people from the family's church routinely gathered in the waiting rooms, in the hallways of the hospital, and out in the parking lots. It was an incredible sight. A prayer chain stretched across the country, and hundreds, maybe even thousands, of people joined in prayer for this young woman. I could feel the strength of their thoughts and prayers behind me.

I gave Atiya's parents a hug and went off to prepare myself for the open-heart surgery.

In the operating room, we put Atiya's heart on cardiopulmonary bypass, so her heart and lungs could be rested and bypassed during the surgery. I removed the mitral valve of Atiya's heart and replaced it with an artificial valve. I took out all the vegetative junk and closed her heart back up. We were in surgery for six hours.

As we wheeled Atiya out of the operating room and into the intensive care unit, I was totally drained. It was a huge feeling of relief, almost like getting off the doomed Apollo 13 spacecraft. But it was tempered by the knowledge that we weren't out of the woods yet.

The next few days were a roller coaster ride of emotion. While most patients come out of their anesthesia within a few hours, Atiya remained unconscious for four anxiety-laden days. During that time, we drained massive amounts of fluids from her. Finally, she started to awaken. When we saw movement and became confident that she was coming to, we removed her breathing tube.

Atiya remained in the hospital for a week. She got steadily stronger, and, incredibly, she showed no sign of brain damage or stroke. She went home a healthy young woman.

Today, Atiya has finished college and earned her degree. Once a year at Christmas, she makes a special trip to the hospital to thank me and to give me a gift. "Part of you is in my heart," she tells me every time.

So often, families think of doctors as saviors. They look to us to redeem their life-or-death situation. Atiya's family was no different.

They put their daughter's life in my hands. But they were looking to someone else for their miracle.

Dr. Jacob DeLaRosa is a cardiothoracic surgeon and chief of cardio-vascular and thoracic surgery at Idaho State University, Portneuf Medical Center in Pocatello, Idaho. His book about heart disease, The Heart Surgery Game Plan, *was published by Misner and Monroe in October 2011.*

19

IN A SMALL POOL OF LIGHT

CRAIG MARTIN, MD, FACOG

OBSTETRICS AND GYNECOLOGY

FRANKLIN, TENNESSEE

We woke up early in Haiti to the sound of pigs and chickens, and the braying of donkeys. The sun wasn't up yet, but we were already sweating. Outside, a long line of patients wrapped around the compound. We brushed ants off our pancakes and syrup, ate quickly, and got ready to face the day.

Patients waited for hours in the sun for their turn to be seen in our clinic. Most walked for many miles. The utter hopelessness of their lives showed in their faces. Against a background of political turmoil, violence, and grinding poverty, they seemed totally beaten down. They appeared almost two-dimensional. Almost no one smiled— there was no expression in their worn faces.

One by one, we attended to people. Our team for this week-long clinic included several specialties—a pediatrician, an internist, a family practitioner, and me, an ob/gyn doctor. We saw patients from about seven in the morning to five o'clock at night. After five o'clock, we began the surgeries we had scheduled for patients we'd seen that day.

On this particular day, one of the other doctors asked me to consult about a patient. Murielle was gaunt and looked to be about 70, although I suspected she was probably no more than 50 years old. A tumor was growing on her left cheek. She had told the doctor, through a translator, that the growth was very painful.

"Can you do anything for her? Can you operate?" my colleague asked.

The request didn't surprise me. OB/GYN doctors are essentially surgeons. Caesarean deliveries, tubal pregnancies, ovarian cysts, endometriosis, fibroid tumors—we're in surgery all the time. And on this trip, I was the only surgeon on the team.

But I had never operated on a person's face before. This was the kind of surgery normally entrusted to an ear-nose-and-throat doctor. I wasn't sure I could accurately remember the anatomy of the face—a textbook would have come in handy!

Not only that, but our operating environment wasn't exactly sterile. We performed our surgeries in a cinder block pavilion that doubled as the clinic. A wooden table served as an operating table. Holes in the cinder block provided the only ventilation, so we had to keep the doors of the pavilion open. People and dogs wandered in and out through the open doors.

Although in the pavilion we were shaded from the oppressive heat, shade was also our enemy. To save fuel, we had to shut down the generator after clinic hours. With no electricity, team members had to hold flashlights and headlamps steady while we huddled over the operating table. Family members crowded in, pressing ever closer as the surgeries progressed, and sweat dripped from our faces.

I thought about what I would need to do. The size of the tumor wasn't a problem. It was probably no more than five centimeters across. It was the location that concerned me.

The tumor was right in the path of Murielle's facial nerve and in the parotid gland that secretes saliva. If I accidentally cut the nerve in the gland of her cheek, her face would sag. She might drool or find it hard to breathe, or she might be unable to smile or even talk.

I knew the risks of this surgery were high, both because of its nature and because of the possibility of infection. But if the surgery went well, it would end this woman's pain and restore her to normalcy.

I explained the risks and benefits of the surgery to the patient and her family. She had come in with three or four generations of family members, everyone from toddlers to great-grandmothers. They all agreed that I should go ahead with the surgery.

I had no general anesthesia to give Murielle, only lidocaine to numb the area. I guessed that the lidocaine would last no more than 30 minutes, so I knew we had to work steadily and efficiently. I glanced around to see that I had what I needed at hand—scalpels, retractors, scissors, sutures, gauze.

There, in a small pool of light, I paused and prayed to God for guidance. I took a deep breath and began.

We cleansed the facial area and covered the rest of Murielle's face, head, and neck with sterile towels. I injected the lidocaine carefully into the skin around the tumor. It couldn't get into a vein or an artery, or Murielle's life would be threatened.

At every step, I told Murielle what I was doing. I had majored in romance languages in college, so I sensed that the translator was accurately conveying my thoughts. I hoped my words would soothe her.

Murielle was stoic. She didn't move a muscle or betray the least bit of fear. The forces that had beaten her down had formed her into a woman who could face anything. She was a rock.

When I was sure the area was numb, I began. I made an incision over the tumor and gently peeled back the skin. I peered into the incision, looking for the facial nerve. Nerves can be tricky to spot. They're white or yellowish in color and look like violin strings. But they're flat and can be mistaken for connective tissue.

I didn't have the cauterizing tools I'd normally have, so the surgical site filled with blood. In the pulpy red area, it was almost impossible to be sure of what I was seeing. But I could rule out the blood vessels, which are more rounded than nerves, and I identified the parotid gland. Gently, I lifted the tumor upward and out of the gland. Then, I saw the facial nerve lying under the tumor.

What a relief! If the nerve had been lying over the tumor or running through it, I would have had to tunnel around it. There would have been a far greater chance of severing the nerve, or any of its tiny branches that snake through the gland. This way I could see exactly where it was.

Working around the nerve, trying not to move it at all, I began to free up the tumor little by little. It's a procedure we call "shelling," and it's like peeling an orange. I worked at it for about an hour until I was certain I had gotten all of it out. In all that time, Murielle didn't flinch—if the lidocaine had worn off, I sure couldn't tell.

Finishing up, I sewed up the incision, bandaged the wound, and gave Murielle a dose of pain medicine. We removed the towels from around her face.

The moment I dreaded had arrived. I turned to the translator.

"Would you ask Murielle how she's doing?" I said. "Would you ask her to please smile for me?"

With the darkness pressing in around us, I waited anxiously while the translator relayed my request.

Murielle looked up at the translator and then at me. Then, slowly, both sides of her mouth turned up into a smile.

In sheer delight, I laughed, and everyone around me began to laugh, too. That smile was such a gift from God—not only for Murielle, but for me. What a moment of grace! It was grace undeserved, but grace humbly accepted.

Dr. Craig Martin practices obstetrics and gynecology at Heritage Women's Center in Franklin, Tennessee, and is a Fellow in the American College of Obstetricians and Gynecologists. He has been on two medical mission trips to Haiti—the best vacations he says he has ever taken. He and his wife, Julia, have four children, Melanie, Mandy, Craig Jr., and Molly.

20

I NEED TO SEE THE BABY!

CHRISTOPHER BLOSS, MD

OBSTETRICS AND GYNECOLOGY

TROY, NEW YORK

Sometimes, because of your own experiences, you become a better doctor. I have something of a reputation as being more like a midwife than a doctor. I really empathize with my patients, especially when something is wrong. That's because I've been there.

My wife Jenn and I had difficulty conceiving. We used fertility treatments for the birth of our first three children. We just knew nothing was ever going to happen the old-fashioned way.

Then, one year, around the holidays, my wife began to have trouble with what we thought was her gall bladder. She had had gall bladder trouble before. The pain, nausea, and fatigue persisted this time and became increasingly intense. Finally, she decided she needed to see her doctor. Before making an appointment, Jenn thought she'd better take a pregnancy test, just to be sure she could take any medication she was prescribed.

I was in the shower when Jenn came into the bathroom. "What do I do next?" she asked, holding out the wand. The test was positive!

I did an ultrasound and determined she was eight weeks pregnant. Something we never thought could happen! Everything looked fine. It didn't look like she needed anything—no betas, no progesterone—to help this baby along.

The pregnancy progressed normally. The lab work all came back good, and the baby's growth was right on target. The baby was active, kicking all along. We had no worries.

As an ob/gyn, I took part in a regular rotation at one of our local hospitals. Once or twice a month, I'd do an overnight shift on the labor and delivery floor, handling emergencies and C-sections.

Sometimes, my wife would come to the hospital with our kids to have dinner with me. On one occasion about two weeks before her due date, we enjoyed dinner together as usual. She was getting the kids ready to leave when our five-year-old, Elizabeth, stopped her.

"I want to see the baby!" she said. "I want to see the baby on the ultrasound."

Elizabeth is normally a laid-back child, not one to seek attention. But on this occasion, she was adamant. Her urgency was unusual. She kept pushing us, even as we tried to dissuade her. We thought there was no reason for it, since the baby was due so soon.

"No, I *need* to see the baby," she said.

Finally, she wore us down. "Okay, fine," I said.

We went into the room with the ultrasound equipment. My wife lay down, and I started the scan. I am very comfortable with sonography. I had performed ultrasounds throughout my residency, and for six months I was the sonographer at my first practice.

At first, looking around, I didn't see much out of the ordinary. But when I began to investigate, I noticed something off about the amniotic fluid. My wife was 38 weeks along—her amniotic fluid should have been much greater than it was. In fact, she should have had about three times as much fluid as I was measuring.

At the same time, I was astonished to find that my measurements indicated a baby at 35 weeks along rather than 38 weeks. The medical term for this anomaly is intrauterine growth restriction. Something was preventing the baby from growing.

I quietly continued the scan. I wasn't saying anything at this point, and my wife noticed.

"Chris, what's wrong?" she asked.

What I was seeing—poor growth and oligohydramnios, or low fluid levels—wasn't good news.

We had to get my wife delivered right away—or our baby was likely to be stillborn.

I called the midwife at our practice. Being the husband and the father, I didn't want to rely on my own advice alone. My partner in the practice was on vacation, so it was just the midwife and me. She agreed that the baby should be delivered as soon as possible.

I made a quick call to the chairman of the department, and he came in to cover the hospital's in-house calls. Jenn's mom, who lives two and a half hours away, started out for our house. Our midwife arrived at the hospital, and I drove the kids home. A couple from our church came over to stay with our children until Jenn's mother arrived. I packed a bag and drove back to the hospital.

Our first step was to induce labor. But it was a tricky business. Jenn had had a C-section with our first child, so we had to be careful about which drugs we used, as some induce very strong contractions.

We started Jenn on a low dose of pitocin. Midway through the night, though, when we saw little progression, we decided we needed to move things along.

The next step would be to break her water. I was reluctant to do this, because fluid cushions the umbilical cord and prevents dangerous changes in the baby's heart rate. But after consulting with the midwife and the department head, I went ahead and broke her water.

As the ultrasound had shown, there was very little fluid.

Jenn's contractions became intense, and labor progressed quickly. She had opted for a water birth and when the time for delivery came, our baby girl, Michaela Grace, was born with no trouble. She was just five pounds, five ounces, but she was clearly healthy.

I was relieved that we had made the right decision. The error rate in determining growth is plus or minus two weeks. It could have turned out that I'd put us through all this for no reason at all. But the small amount of amniotic fluid confirmed our decision.

The reality is that we averted a terrible fate. Babies in this situation have a fourfold increase in stillbirth. If it it hadn't been for for our daughter Elizabeth and her insistence on seeing the baby that night, we could have been among those statistics. Yet today Michaela is doing fine—she's tiny, only in the tenth percentile in terms of weight and height—but she's a spunky little person.

I don't know why God chose to bless us in this way. I have delivered stillborn babies and babies that are too premature to survive. I am moved to pray for every woman whose delivery I attend. "God, let her know you are there for her," I pray. "Give her strength and energy."

It was a privilege to help deliver our baby. And I'm not the only one who feels this way. Elizabeth is pleased to have played a part in the safe delivery of her sister. She is a very humble child, yet to this day she is proud to tell us, "I got to be used by God!" To me, the experience speaks to God's power and to his providential love.

Dr. Christopher Bloss is an obstetrician and gynecologist in practice with Community Care Physicians of Troy, New York. He has been practicing medicine since 2004. He and his wife, Jennifer, have five children, Alexandra, Elizabeth, Nathaniel, Michaela, and Josephine.

21

THE RICHEST MAN

WALTER LARIMORE, MD

FAMILY MEDICINE

COLORADO SPRINGS, COLORADO

After spending his life in the jungles of Africa teaching, preaching, and ministering, John returned to Kissimmee, Florida, to retire at age 72. His return was forced by what he called "a considerable thorn in the flesh."

A number of men in his family had suffered and died from congestive heart failure. Now, multiple parasitic infections had complicated John's own heart condition and the renal difficulties associated with it.

Because of John's frequent need for medical care, we became good friends. He was a man of unpretentious faith and unadorned words. He had few worldly goods and no earthly estate of any consequence. Many would consider his life plain, even unsuccessful. I found him, however, to be rich with experience—a treasure trove of wonderful memories and stories. He had a wisdom based on the crucible of life experiences and the Scriptures, which he cherished.

The moments I spent with him were fruitful and always too short. His timing was impeccable. He seemed to be in the office whenever my partners and I were discouraged or down. We fretted more about his health than he did.

John always told us he thought we lived in a society with too many luxuries, and that many of us had forgotten the purity of the basics. He loved to say that America has too much fast food, too many fast lanes, too many shortcuts, and too much instant gratification. He often quoted Max Lucado, saying, "America is the only country in the world with a mountain called 'Rushmore.'" He encouraged us to differentiate between what most people consider to be wealth—money, securities, houses, possessions, positions, and power—and what he felt made up true wealth: relationships, service, wisdom, love, joy, peace, wonderful memories, and an abiding faith.

I cared for him for three years, until at age 75, he found himself in our local hospital with complications stemming from an overgrown prostate.

In the hospital, I drained his bloated bladder and brought his heart and kidney failure into some sort of equilibrium, but his prostate needed attention beyond my skill level. So I asked for a consultation from Dr. Frank, a skilled urologist.

This colleague of mine was generally believed to be the richest man in our town. His car cost more than most people's houses, his monthly mortgage was more than my annual one, and he seemed to take great pride in showing off his numerous and expensive possessions.

The nurse who was caring for John told me about the urologic consultation. Dr. Frank pompously entered the room while John and his wife, Beth, were praying over their breakfast. Rather than interrupting—as would be his usual approach—he stood quietly by. When John looked up, he apologized for making the doctor wait.

"Humph," sneered the doctor, regarding the full-liquid meal. "If that was all I had to eat, I don't think I'd feel very thankful."

John smiled and replied, "Well, it really is quite enough for us." His wife nodded in agreement. Then John said: "I'm pleased to meet you. I've heard so much about you. I'm glad you came by this morning, because I want to tell you about a dream I had last night."

Dr. Frank and the nurse looked on, amused.

John gazed out the window across the neighboring field as he related his vision: "The dream began with light and beauty all around me, and I felt so peaceful. Then I heard a quiet voice say to me, 'The richest man in town will die tonight.'"

Dr. Frank was stunned, and for a moment he was speechless. As John turned his soft, brown eyes to look at this younger man, Dr. Frank exclaimed, "Dreams . . . rubbish! Let's take a look at what we can do something about—your prostate problem."

Dr. Frank performed a thorough exam. When he left, John turned to the nurse and his wife and said, "I pray the Lord will have mercy on him."

As I found out later, John's warning reverberated in Dr. Frank's mind all morning. *Die tonight?* he thought. *Rubbish! Absolute rubbish!* He felt that the best thing to do was to forget about it—but he couldn't. It plagued him the entire day. He found himself wondering about the substernal pain he had had last last week during his divorce deposition and the recurrent heartburn he had experienced during his most recent malpractice trial.

Could these signs be a warning of something more serious? His thoughts tormented him throughout the day. Finally, after his last patient, he jumped in his sports car and came to my office.

My receptionist told me he had entered the office that evening unannounced, demanding and expecting us—as he usually did—to drop everything to examine his malady of the day. He was waiting at my office door, obviously distressed. Before I examined him, he told me the whole story.

It was unusual for Dr. Frank to exhibit fear. I did a complete examination. Apart from the smoker's rhonchi, which cleared with a cough, the results were normal. With that reassurance sloughed aside, he demanded a chest X-ray, a complete blood count, and an electro-cardiogram. All tests were normal.

I thought to myself, *Other than your chronic stress, acute anxiety, recurrent dyspepsia, dysfunctional family relationships, misplaced priori-ties, obvious spiritual needs, possible masked depression, and tobacco abuse, you're fine.* But I had the fortitude only to say, "You're as healthy as a horse, at least physically. But it wouldn't hurt to begin to take care of yourself physically *and* spiritually."

Dr. Frank seemed reassured but wanted to be certain. "Cut to the chase," he said sharply. "What's the bottom line?"

I sensed his urgency and said, "There is no way you're going to die tonight. However, if you don't stop smoking and begin to take care of yourself . . . " I began the admonishment, but he didn't allow me to finish.

Having received the reassurance he had come for, and after having gruffly silenced the sermon, he muttered, "Thanks, Walt. I really appreciate the help." Then he left, confident that his health was as permanent as his considerable skills and wealth. But to me it was obvious that he was embarrassed to have been, as he said, "so fool-ishly upset by a debilitated man's delusional dream."

The phone call came at about 4 A.M. It took a moment for me to wake up as I heard the distress in the voice on the other end of the line.

"Walt, I can't believe it. I woke up and found him dead. He wasn't breathing. He didn't make any noise. He didn't even wake me. He died in his sleep. When I dozed off, he seemed to be sleeping so peace-fully. Now, he's gone."

It was Beth, relaying the bad news that John had died.

I was stunned. I couldn't believe it. John had seemed stable when I saw him earlier that evening in the hospital. Then I remembered his dream and his vivid prediction.

Indeed, the richest man in Kissimmee had died that night.

Dr. Walter Larimore is a family physician who practices in Colorado. He is a medical journalist with over 700 articles, editorials, and monographs to his credit, and he has hosted numerous television, Internet, and radio programs. Dr. Larimore has written or co-written thirty books, including his best-selling Bryson City series about his early years as a family physi-cian in the Smoky Mountains of North Carolina. Dr. Larimore and his wife, Barb, have two adult children, two grandchildren, and an adopted cat named Jack. "The Richest Man" was published as "The Wealthiest Man in Kissimmee" in Focus on the Family's Physician magazine (July/August 1995). His daily health news blog is at www.DrWalt.com/blog and his daily devotional blog is at www.DrWalt.com/devotional.

NOTE: About six months after this incident, Dr. Frank and I shared a meal. We had a long discussion about beginning a personal relationship with God. He bowed his head and prayed to ask Christ to enter his life. A year later, he passed away suddenly. I'm looking forward to seeing him in heaven. —WL

22

A Hunter's Cry

James Foulkes, MD
Missionary Medicine
Boone, North Carolina

One of the unwritten job descriptions for a doctor at Mukinge Hospital in Zambia, where I practiced medicine for 38 years, was to provide meat for the inpatients. The hospital served protein-rich meat once a week to our patients, which at any time could number 160 to 200 people.

Of course, we couldn't just go down to the local supermarket and order our meat. We had to hunt it ourselves. At the time, Africa's animals weren't endangered as they are now. Kasempa District alone was home to more than ten thousand elephants. Nothing quite fit the bill—or the freezer—like a huge bull elephant. The meat from just one elephant could last us a year.

So, one day my hunting partner, Ba Kalima, and I hopped into my dune buggy and headed for Kafue National Park. We had hunted together many times through the years and deeply respected each other's skills.

Ba Kalima was the pastor of Mukinge Church and the district superintendent for sixty mission churches. He was an expert tracker and a master of bush survival. He knew what berries you could eat and when fruit from certain trees was edible. He could look at a bruised piece of grass sticking up from rock-hard ground in the dry season and tell you if an elephant had stepped on it. He could even tell you whether the elephant had stepped on it thirty minutes ago or three hours ago. I brought to the hunt my skill with a .458 rifle.

About 35 miles from the hospital, we came to a large open plain. A herd of 26 elephants stood in the middle, about a half mile from the tree line. A huge bull stood in the middle of the herd, his back a full two feet higher than the others. He was exactly what we were looking for—but to get closer, we'd have to cross the open plain. Was it worth the risk?

As a bush surgeon, I had conducted many a postmortem on people killed by elephants, not to mention lions, leopards, and Cape buffalo. Once, I was called on to examine the remains of a man who had been smashed repeatedly against a tree by a jumbo elephant, disarticulated until his body was nothing more than parts.

But here in front of us was five tons of meat—meat that we desperately needed.

Kalima and I began to crawl Army-style across the plain, inch by painful inch on our bellies, propelled by our elbows over the black grass stubble. Elephants don't have very good eyesight, but they have a highly developed sense of smell, so every minute or so I stopped and shook out a tiny bit of flour from an empty cartridge to make sure that the wind was either dead still or blowing toward us. A sudden change of wind could doom us.

We snaked along until we were a hundred yards from the herd. At this point, if you can muster up enough saliva to lick a postage stamp, you are definitely overconfident! But to get a humane shot, we had to drag ourselves another fifty yards closer.

Finally, we got within range, and the bull presented a full side view of his massive head. I aimed and squeezed off a shot. The mammoth bull dropped with a tremendous thud. Success!

Still, we stayed where we were to make sure we had gotten off a kill shot. We thought we had. But we were wrong. Just a few minutes later, the big bull staggered to his feet like a punch-drunk boxer. He had only been knocked unconscious.

The wounded bull started bellowing, and absolute bedlam broke out. The entire herd, inflamed and trumpeting madly, began stomping their feet, kicking up a dust storm that swirled over our heads. They raised their trunks in unison, sampling the air to locate their enemy.

Kalima and I had been accompanied on the hunt by five helpers who were huddled together at the tree line. Frightened by the agitated herd, they bolted in the other direction. The elephants picked up their movement and began charging at top speed in a solid phalanx.

Kalima and I were in the direct path of seventy tons of charging elephants.

We knew we were dead. But our survival instincts forced us up. We knew full well that even the fastest sprinter had no chance of outrunning an elephant. But it seemed better to scramble to our feet and run rather than be trampled to death lying down.

While we were running, I glanced over my shoulder and was shocked to find that the herd had already halved our lead. With the fearsome shudder of the ground reverberating up through our legs, my prayer at that moment is just as vivid to me today as it was then.

"Lord, I'm coming home!" I cried.

At that precise moment, the thundering herd, now only a few steps behind us—trumpets blaring at ear-splitting decibels—suddenly turned sharply to the right, almost as if by command.

We didn't stop or even slow down. We just kept on running for the trees. For ten minutes, we listened as the herd crashed through the dense forest, stomping on bush and tree, the elephants roaring as they raced further and further away from us.

My chest heaved as I struggled to breathe. As soon as I could get words out, I turned to Kalima. "What happened?" I asked. Still catching his breath, my old friend answered me.

"Man disobeys God, but animals never do," he said. "When God speaks, they listen. The Lord told them to turn right and they did."

I have never doubted Kalima's words. It was clear to us that the Lord is ultimately in control of the events of heaven and earth. Being saved from imminent death magnified my trust in God. I thank him for the miraculous extension of life he granted us that day.

Dr. James Foulkes practiced medicine in Zambia for 38 years. He and his wife, Marilyn, were stationed at Mukinge Hospital under the direction of the South Africa General Mission. Marilyn and two of their children died in Africa. In 1997, he retired to Boone, North Carolina. The following year, he received the Award for Excellence in Medical Missions, presented by Franklin Graham. Today, he and his wife, Martha, have three daughters and eight grandchildren. "A Hunter's Cry" is excerpted and adapted with permission from Dr. Foulkes's book, To Africa with Love: A Bush Doc's Story *(Evangel Publishing House, 2005), written with Joe Lacy.*

23

THE GREATEST GENERATION

STEPHEN R. ELLISON, MD

FORMER U.S. ARMY OFFICER

EMERGENCY MEDICINE

LAMPASAS, TEXAS

I am a doctor specializing in emergency medicine in the emergency departments of two military Level 1 trauma centers in San Antonio, Texas. Because of these two large military medical centers, San Antonio has the largest military retiree population in the world. Here, we care for military personnel as well as civilians.

As a military doctor in training for my specialty, I work long hours and the pay is less than glamorous. One tends to become jaded by the long hours, the lack of sleep, food and family contact, and the endless parade of human suffering passing before you. The arrival of another ambulance does not mean more pay, only more work.

Most often, it is a victim from a motor vehicle crash. Or, a person of dubious character who has been shot or stabbed. With our large military retiree population, it is often a nursing home patient. Even with my enlisted service and minimal combat experience in Panama prior to medical school, I have caught myself groaning when the ambulance brought in yet another sick, elderly person from one of the local retirement centers that cater to military retirees.

I had never stopped to think of what citizens of this age group represented.

I was deeply touched by the movie "Saving Private Ryan" about World War II's D-Day invasion—not so much by the carnage depicted in the horrifying scenes of the invasion itself, but by the single scene of an elderly survivor at a Normandy graveside. There, he asks his wife whether he has been a good man.

I realized at that moment that I had seen these same men and women coming through my emergency departments, and I had not realized what magnificent sacrifices they made. The acts of honor and courage they performed for me and for everyone else who has lived on this planet since the end of that conflict are priceless.

Situation permitting, I now try to ask my patients about their experiences. They would never bring up the subject without the inquiry. I have been privileged to hear an amazing array of experiences recounted in the brief minutes allowed in an emergency department encounter. These experiences have revealed the incredible individuals I have had the honor of serving in a medical capacity, many on their last admission to the hospital.

There was the frail, elderly woman who quietly reassured my young enlisted medic, who was trying unsuccessfully to start an IV line in her arm. She was what we call a "hard stick," but she remained calm and poised despite her illness and the multiple needle-sticks into her fragile veins. As the medic made yet another attempt, I noticed a number tattooed across her forearm. I touched it with one finger and looked into her eyes. She simply said, "Auschwitz."

Many people would have loudly and openly berated this young medic for his many painful attempts to insert a needle. How different was the response from this person who had truly known unspeakable suffering.

Also, I recall the long-retired colonel who as a young Navy officer had parachuted from his burning plane over a Pacific island held by the Japanese. Now an octogenarian, he had cut his head in a fall at home where he lived alone. His CT scan and suturing had been delayed until after midnight by the usual parade of high-priority ambulance patients. Still spry for his age, he asked to use the phone to call a taxi to take him home, but then realized the ambulance had brought him to the hospital without his wallet.

The retired colonel asked if he could use the phone to make a long distance call to his daughter, who lived 70 miles away. With great pride, we told him that he could not, as he'd done plenty for his country and the least we could do was get him a taxi home, and that we would gladly pay for it ourselves. My only regret was that my shift wouldn't end for several hours, and I couldn't drive him myself.

I was there the night Master Sergeant Roy Benavidez came through the emergency department for the last time. He was very sick. I was not the doctor taking care of him, but I walked to his bedside and took his hand. I said nothing. He was so sick he didn't know I was there. But I'd read his Congressional Medal of Honor citation and wanted to shake his hand. He died a few days later.

One after the other, they came before us: the gentleman who served with Merrill's Marauders, the survivor of the Bataan Death March, the survivor of D-Day at Omaha Beach, the 101-year-old World War I veteran, the former POW held in frozen North

Korea, the former Special Forces medic, the former Vietnam Corps commander.

I remember these citizens. I may still groan when yet another ambulance comes in, but now I am aware of what an honor it is to serve these men and women. It has become my personal endeavor to make sure the nurses and young enlisted medics who work with me are aware of these amazing individuals when we encounter them in our emergency department. Their enthusiastic response to these citizens has made me think that perhaps all is not lost.

My experiences with these courageous men and women have solidified my belief that we are losing an incredible generation, and we don't fully realize and appreciate what we are losing. We should all take the time to stop and remember what they have earned for us.

Dr. Stephen R. Ellison resigned from the U.S. Army in 2004 as a major with more than 12 years of combined officer and enlisted service. He was an enlisted medic in the 1st Battalion, 75th Ranger Regiment, and also served as program director for the Joint Special Operations Medical Training Center at Fort Bragg, North Carolina, where he supervised the training of enlisted medical personnel for Army Special Forces, Rangers, Air Force Pararescue, Marine Corps Marine RECON, and Navy SEAL units. Dr. Ellison continues to care for military retirees and dependents in the Central Texas area. He and his wife, Marta, have two children, Michaela and Jonathan. "The Greatest Generation" was adapted with permission from an e-mail Dr. Ellison sent to a friend in April 2000.

24

TODAY'S SPECIAL IS . . .

CRAIG HILDRETH, MD
MEDICAL ONCOLOGY
ST. LOUIS, MISSOURI

I love eating in hospital cafeterias. I feel sad that many of them—
probably as the result of a surprise visit by the hospital president—no
longer resemble a Soviet-era East German department store. This is
a shame. Don't you pine for the return of mauve carpeting? Cinder
block walls and prison-style picnic tables—now, there's a décor we
can all appreciate. Little touches that bring back memories of elemen-
tary school!

One difference between hospital cafeterias and fancy restaurants
is that the cafeteria caters to a captive audience. This is blatantly
unfair and leads to the excessive consumption of steamed okra and
tri-colored meats. On the other hand, restaurants are not required
to post a mission statement. If asked, I would be happy to shorten
the mission statement of a hospital cafeteria to a blessedly direct
philosophy of service and compassion: "Eat up!"

The cafeteria does a great job of filling stomachs, but there's no
question that it fails in the category of "Most Enticing Entrée." A dripping glob of biscuits and gravy will never win a culinary contest against

a tender lattice of baby arugula drizzled with aged balsamic vinegar. What is it that prevents a hospital from serving sesame-encrusted Chilean sea bass on a bed of basmati rice with a Thai curry reduction?

Ah, well. Who has time to savor such lofty cuisine, anyway, when the waiting room is filled with ailing, frowning grandmothers?

Just as a fisherman learns which lure will bring him the best luck, I have decided that choosing the same lunch day after day—a turkey sandwich, no mayo—is the best way to stay sane in the cafeteria.

Boring, you say? Yes, it is—but if I stick to my low-fat, low-cholesterol, low-sodium, low-pleasure meal, at least I know my arteries are sighing with relief. The same cannot be said for some of my acquaintances who pile on the victuals as if they were in the dining hall of the Titanic.

The hospital cafeteria is not just where I pick up my parsimonious menu selection. It is where I go to conjure up distant but comforting memories of milk mustaches, soggy bologna sandwiches packed in Gilligan's Island lunch boxes, and silly grade school jokes. It's where I go to replenish my body and brain before reluctantly returning to the long shadows of the afternoon.

When you boil away all of the skin and fat of the hospital cafeteria menu, you discover that the essential ingredient for a pleasant visit there is not the fare—it is the patrons. I feel sorry for doctors who avoid the dining hall, afraid of getting stuck sitting next to a cranky surgeon, or some drowsy unidentified soul who suddenly belches and starts shoveling in fried potatoes like Grandma stuffing the Thanksgiving turkey. They are missing out on what high school counselors gently call "life lessons."

What makes my time in the hospital eatery satisfying is the opportunity to engage my colleagues in lively conversation, such as griping about the latest directive handed down from an administrator who apparently resides on Mount Olympus. As an oncologist, I also get peppered with queries such as "Hey, Craig—what went wrong with that patient I sent you last week?" (Gulp!)

A cafeteria visit with my esteemed colleagues today is a far cry from the days when I was an underfed medical student grabbing an automat sandwich and an apple while galloping down the hallway to Gross Anatomy, my piggy bank—and myself—thus the poorer.

These days, I can sit with my fellow laborers for hours rehashing last night's sports scores or lampooning any poor souls unfortunate enough to be out of earshot. (Doctors do gossip, you know.) Such camaraderie certainly brightens the mood—if not the food—for all of us, nudging the sluggish afternoon to keep moving.

Beware, though, as lunch in the hospital cafeteria can unwittingly steal away those same afternoon hours. If we doctors linger too long over our empty plates, a fairy-sized nurse will inevitably fly into our ears and whisper softly:

"Get back to work, you slobs!"

Dr. Craig Hildreth practices medical oncology in the greater St. Louis, Missouri, area. "Today's Special Is . . . " is adapted with permission from the multi-post entry "A Trip to St. Elsewhere" on Dr. Hildreth's former blog, The Cheerful Oncologist. *He and his wife, Elizabeth, have three teenage children, which explains a lot.*

25

ALONE IN A BLIZZARD

VISHNU "CHUCK" MULAY, MD

GENERAL SURGERY

FULTON, ILLINOIS

There are a lot of lessons a young surgeon learns. One of the biggest to come my way happened outside the operating room in the dead of winter many years ago.

Back then I was practicing at a small hospital in Manchester, Iowa, about 19 miles west of my home in Dyersville, an easy half-hour drive on a two-lane country road. Easy in good weather, that is. I had a hernia surgery scheduled at 7:30 one morning. The patient was a young boy.

The surgery didn't worry me so much, but the weather did. I looked out my window before I went to sleep the night before. Snow was coating the trees in our neighborhood. The road was almost completely white. *Hope I can get to the hospital tomorrow*, I thought, vowing to get an extra-early start.

First thing in the morning, I looked out the window again. The snow had slowed. *I can make it*, I thought. I dressed, threw on my coat, and hopped into the car.

The road was icy but manageable. Then, halfway to the hospital, the tires lost their grip. I tried to steer, but the car just slid . . . right off the road. *Bam!* White burst across the windshield. I'd ditched into a huge snowbank.

Shaken, I got out of the car, pulling my coat tight. The temperature was below zero, and the light snow had become a full-blown blizzard. I looked around. No cars in either direction. Not at this hour, not in this weather. The closest town was miles away. I'd succumb to hypothermia before I got anywhere. For the first time in my adult life, I was truly terrified. *God, if you really are there, I could use some help.*

Just then, I saw headlights in the distance. A four-wheel-drive Scout. I waved frantically. The vehicle pulled over. Inside was an elderly farm couple. "Need a ride?" the man asked. His wife offered me a cup of coffee from their thermos.

"Thank you so much," I said, climbing into the backseat of the Scout.

"What are you doing on the road in this weather?" the woman asked.

"I'm a doctor," I said, "and I'm headed to the hospital in Manchester."

"So are we!" said the man. "Our grandson is having surgery today. Maybe you know the surgeon. His name is Dr. Mulay."

Dr. Mulay is a board-certified general surgeon born in India, who practiced in Iowa and Illinois until his retirement. Earlier in his career, he was deputy chief surgeon of the U.S. Marine Hospital in Norfolk, Virginia. A widower, he has two children, Joe and Tara, and his wife, Patricia, has three children, John, Jackie, and Stephanie. Together, they are grandparents to Alexis, Misha, Jessica, Julian, and Nick.

26

A SECRET SIGN

ROBERT OH, MD

LT. COL., U.S. ARMY MEDICAL CORPS

FAMILY MEDICINE

HONOLULU, HAWAII

And hope does not disappoint us,
because God has poured out his love into our hearts
by the Holy Spirit, whom he has given us.

ROMANS 5:5

After I returned from a deployment to Kosovo, I was on the faculty of the residency clinic at Madigan Army Medical Center in Tacoma, Washington. I was studying for a master's degree and also seeing a few patients at the clinic.

One morning, a woman arrived at the clinic with a complaint that startled me—she said she was crying tears of blood. I'd never seen this condition before, so I thought maybe it was an exaggeration, or something different than what it seemed.

When I walked into the exam room, I could see right away that my patient had indeed been crying. Sarah's eyes were bloodshot, and she held a wad of tissues in her hand.

"I've been sad," Sarah said. "I've been crying blood."

As she told me this, I could see bloody tears begin to form in her eyes.

I examined Sarah and was convinced she was right. Her tears were in fact mixed with blood.

"Why are you so sad?" I asked Sarah.

I sat down, and Sarah told me her heartbreaking story.

She was in her 40s and had two daughters. One daughter had been pregnant, but she lost her baby in the second trimester, long after Sarah had formed an attachment to her much-anticipated grandchild. Shortly after that loss, her other daughter and her son-in-law were killed in a horrific auto accident.

"I've been crying for the last couple of weeks," Sarah said. And who wouldn't have been? Her losses were tremendous.

Now, I know there is a medical explanation for the phenomenon of bloody tears. If a person has been crying very hard for a long time, the capillaries of the conjunctiva, the lining of the inner lids, can break and leak blood into the tears. If Sarah had come in to see me a year ago, I might have simply told her this, prescribed medication and counseling, and sent her on her way.

But I had been on a faith journey the last few years, beginning with my time in Kosovo and later when I was stationed in Germany. My heart was softened, and I was open to seeking spiritual meaning in the circumstances of life. I wondered if Sarah might be, too.

"It's natural that after tragedies as great as yours that you would cry as hard as you have," I said. "Jesus himself cried when he grieved, and the Bible says he was in such agony before his crucifixion that he sweat great drops of blood in the Garden of Gethsemane."

When I spoke those words, a sweeping change came over Sarah's face. A look of wonder arose in her eyes, and her entire complexion brightened.

"I've thought about that, too," she said.

I asked Sarah whether I could pray with her that she would find hope and comfort in her suffering, and she said she would like that.

After we finished, Sarah said she wanted to tell me something she had not told anyone, something she had not dared tell anyone, for fear of being ridiculed.

"I accompanied my daughter to her ultrasound early in her pregnancy," she said. "As I watched, I saw a cross appear on the screen. I don't know what it meant, but I am sure I saw a sign of the cross."

Now, ultrasound images can be blurry at best, but I did not dissuade Sarah from her vision.

"Perhaps you experienced a sign that everything will be okay, that although you are deeply wounded, you will come through this time of grief and sorrow," I said. "Perhaps this encounter with the cross was part of God's plan to prepare you to face your suffering."

As I spoke, I could see a look of relief come over Sarah's face. She had kept her vision bottled up inside her out of fear that no one would believe her, but now she was being validated in her suffering and relieved of her burden.

Sarah nodded her head. "Yes, I agree," she said.

And then, just as bloody tears of sorrow had once sprung to her eyes, tears of joy now began to stream down her face.

I can medicalize this encounter—as a physician, I can diagnose the physical cause of a person's malady. But, truly, medicine is practiced best when it touches the soul and reveals the glory of God.

Dr. Robert Oh, Lieutenant Colonel, U.S. Army Medical Corps, is director of the family medicine residency program at Tripler Army Medical Center in Honolulu, Hawaii. During his Army career, he has been deployed to Kosovo as Officer-in-Charge of the Camp Monteith Troop Medical Clinic, 299th Logistics Task Force, 1st Infantry Division, in support of Task Force Falcon, and to Germany as a family physician at the Darmstadt Health Clinic. He and his wife, Connie, have one daughter, Emily.

27

THE WOUNDED HEALER

RANDALL WRIGHT, MD

NEUROLOGY

THE WOODLANDS, TEXAS

The good physician treats the disease;

the great physician treats the patient who has the disease.

SIR WILLIAM OSLER

One day during my residency, we were coming to the close of a long shift—an endless, wearying parade of patients. All of us were ready to head out the door, but I stopped one of my attending physicians to ask for his opinion.

"I have one more patient I'd like you to see," I said. "He has a newly enlarged lymph node in his neck, and he says he's been more tired than usual. It might just be the flu, but I'm wondering if there could be something more."

"OK, where's the patient? I'll take a look at him," my attending said.

"You're looking at him."

I was 27 years old and had just graduated from medical school. I was starting my internal medicine internship, and just a week earlier

I had asked my sweetheart to marry me. (She said yes!) I was excited about my future.

When I began to have the symptoms I described to the doctor, I didn't think much of it. But it just so happens that in the very same month, we were studying oncology—the branch of medicine that deals with tumors—and I was seeing some patients with symptoms similar to mine.

After examining me, the doctor said he thought we ought to do a biopsy of the lymph node as well as a bone marrow biopsy. The result was what I had suspected and feared: Hodgkin's lymphoma. Cancer.

When I got the news, I was stunned. All my plans for the future grew dim. I didn't even know if I had a future. Leaving the hospital that day, I knelt down on the sidewalk and prayed out loud.

"Lord, I know you can get me through anything," I said. "Whatever you have in store for me, I know that you will never let me down."

Over dinner that night with my fiancé, I broke the news to her. We both cried. Then I took a deep breath and said the hardest thing I'd ever had to say in my life.

"You're young, Crystal. You have your whole life ahead of you," I said. "You don't have to do this—it's not your cross to bear. I don't expect you to marry me."

Her reply was swift and sweet. "Of course I'll marry you. There's no question," she said. "I love you, and God will help get us through this together."

My treatment was a course of radiation to the neck and chest area. I was fortunate not to need chemotherapy. My days became hectic. I would see patients in my morning clinic, and then run out to the radiation oncology department down the street to receive my own radiation treatments. I would often get calls from the emergency room and have to manage patients over the phone while on the radiation table. When my treatment was done, I would drive back to my clinic and continue seeing patients.

I'm pleased to say I never missed a day of work, but the going was tough. I was so exhausted that I could barely get out of bed. Food burned going down, and I had continual heartburn. My stomach was so upset that it was often a struggle not to lose my lunch. Sometimes, while I was in an exam room with a patient, I would have to excuse myself quickly and make a dash for the nearest bathroom.

The attending physicians at the hospital watched out for me. If a call came over to go to a code, they'd literally push me aside. "No you don't!" they'd say. "You need to stay away from this patient—you don't need to catch any infections."

By God's grace, I got through the treatment and today, 15 years later, I am cancer free. But I learned a powerful lesson in my illness. Cancer turned this doctor into a patient. I wore the flimsy hospital gown and suffered the embarrassment of exposure. I submitted to treatment, fearful and alone on the radiation table.

The experience transformed my approach to medicine. Cancer made me a more compassionate doctor. I realized that cancer or no cancer, I was still Randy Wright. I wasn't just Patient X.

As a doctor, I've slowed down, and I listen more. You may have a longer wait for your appointment with me, but that's because I'm in with another patient, listening to every word she says, assuring her of my concern. Being the wounded healer has allowed me to connect to the heart of my patients.

Dr. Randall Wright is director of the Neurovascular Institute at Conroe Regional Medical Center and medical director of the Stroke Recovery Care Unit of Health South Rehabilitation Hospital, The Woodlands, Texas. His practice focuses on general neurological disorders with a special emphasis on epilepsy, stroke, and sleep disorders. He has recently published a book, co-authored by Chicken Soup for the Soul *writer David Tabatsky, titled* The Wright Choice: Your Family's Prescription for Healthy Eating, Modern Fitness, and Saving Money *(Intouch Media Health Network, 2011). He writes about health and fitness at his website,* The Wright Choice RX *(www.TheWrightChoiceRX.com). He and his wife, Crystal, have two very active boys affectionately known as "the Wright brothers."*

28

A Cry in Cyberspace

Sylvia Campbell, MD, FACS
General Surgery
Tampa, Florida

On New Year's Eve of 2000, I was relaxing at home in a recliner, with my 15-year-old daughter reading on the floor next to me. I opened my laptop to check my e-mail, expecting to see holiday greetings from friends and family members. In my inbox, I spotted an e-mail from an address I didn't recognize. The subject line read: "Appeal for sponsorship in heart surgery."

Wary of spam, I almost didn't open the e-mail. I was just about to hit the delete key. But something stopped me. I opened the e-mail and began to read.

"Dear Doctor Sylvia, I am a 15-year-old girl in Uganda," it began. "I am a total orphan. My father died five years ago and my mother three years ago.

"Doctors identified that I have a hole in my heart. I feel pain and fatigue whenever I carry out any tedious activity. I have grown very thin for my age and I find it difficult to walk long distances.

"There is no facility for a heart operation in Uganda. I am, there-fore, kindly appealing for your kind consideration to sponsor me in any way possible. God bless you in your efforts to save the needy."

The young girl's name was Martha. She lived in the village of Papoli with her aunt and uncle after both of her parents had died of AIDS.

How had Martha gotten my name? I wondered. I had gone on many trips to Haiti, but I had never been to Uganda. I was intrigued.

Five years earlier, while I was in Haiti, I had treated a baby who was severely burned after falling into a vat of boiling water. We needed to get the boy to the United States right away. But a hurricane had knocked out our communications equipment. Undeterred, one of our nurses climbed a CB tower and straightened out an antenna that had been bent in the storm, so that we could make a call. A very brave woman indeed! We arranged for a UN helicopter to transport the baby to Florida.

I wrote an article about the case for an international surgical journal, and it seems that a doctor in Martha's village had seen it. He passed my e-mail address along to her, and with all the faith of a child, she had reached out to me. Incredibly, this girl who was so sick she could barely walk across a room had walked eight miles to an Internet café to send me an e-mail.

What could I do? Perhaps it was the fact of my own healthy, beau-tiful daughter snuggled at my feet that made the girl's plight so poi-gnant to me. I resolved that I could not let this little girl die.

I began to hunt around to see what could be done. Through the Rotary's Gift of Life program, I found that the girl's heart surgery could be done at St. Joseph's Hospital in Tampa, where I work. My church raised the funds needed to buy plane tickets for Martha and her uncle to travel to the United States.

A few months later, I waited at the airport for Martha's flight to touch down. The plane landed, and the passengers started streaming down the jetway. I looked anxiously for Martha and her uncle, but did not see them. I began to worry that they hadn't come. But finally, there they were—the last people to leave the plane!

Martha and her uncle stayed with us for about seven weeks. Her heart disease was more severe than we had thought—she had an atrial septal defect and actually had four or five holes between the chambers of her heart. When I heard her diagnosis, I was relieved that we had acted. Without treatment, Martha would not have lived long.

I accompanied Martha as she was brought into the operating room for her open-heart surgery. Standing scrubbed in on the case, I watched the beauty of the dance that was the cardiac surgery team, each member an integral part of a ballet that took place with form and grace. In the pediatric cardiac surgery unit that night, Martha smiled weakly at me, and I assured her that she would be fine.

Martha came home from the hospital soon after, and gradually she gained strength, buoyed by the cards and visits of people from our church and our community. Eventually, she began to smile and to laugh, and in time she ventured out with us, spending a day at Disney, attending school with my daughter Chelsey, and going on outings with people from the Rotary Club.

Martha began calling me "mama," and everyone fell in love with her. Our hearts were touched by the plight of Uganda, a poor country whose people have been ravaged by endless civil wars and rebellions. The AIDS epidemic has decimated an entire generation, leaving behind orphaned children like Martha. Africa, once an unknown continent to us, was made personal by the wonder and beauty of these new friends in our lives.

After Martha returned to Uganda, our church raised scholarship money for her education and she became a teacher. The church also helped 15 other children in Martha's extended family get an education.

But it wasn't long before the church wanted to do even more, and people from other churches and in the community began asking for ways to help. Access to clean water was a real need in Papoli, so we helped the village build wells. Housing for orphans and widows was another area of greet need, so we partnered with them to build traditional huts with straw roofs.

Eventually, we created a nonprofit organization called Village Partners International. We partner with the Haitian and Ugandan people in their own villages to address health, education, housing, and business needs in an independent and sustainable way. We have started programs that provide food for schoolchildren and for hospital patients.

In Papoli, we have helped build 81 two-room homes with plaster walls and corrugated metal roofs for households headed by widows and children. Most recently, we partnered with Papoli to build a medical clinic. The village divided itself into seven groups, each taking on the job of making 10,000 bricks for the building. The clinic is staffed and operated solely by Ugandans.

All of this became possible because one day, in desperation, a 15-year-old girl sent an e-mail out into cyberspace.

I could never have imagined what God would do because I happened to be in Haiti, because a nurse climbed a CB tower, because a village doctor read a medical journal, and because a sick little girl had faith that someone could help her. It is such a miracle. I am humbled to be a small part of this incredible adventure.

Dr. Sylvia Campbell is a general surgeon in private practice who treats primarily breast cancer patients. She is a Fellow in the American College of Surgeons. In addition to her work at St. Joseph's Hospital, she volunteers her time for Village Partners International and at the Judeo Christian Health Clinic in Tampa, Florida, for which she is president of the board. She has been leading medical mission trips to Haiti and Uganda for 15 years, and she volunteered in Mississippi after Hurricane Katrina. She and her husband, Bob, have three children, Chelsey, Meaghan, and Ross.

29

GOD'S PERFECT TIMING

DOLAPO BABALOLA, MD

FAMILY MEDICINE

ATLANTA, GEORGIA

What is impossible with men is possible with God.

LUKE 18:27

On September 18, 2009, I woke up declaring, "Lord, you have to come through for me today!"

That day, I was scheduled to interview at the U.S. Consulate in Lagos, Nigeria, for my working visa, which had expired two months earlier.

I had lived in the United States since 2001 and was on the faculty of the Department of Family Medicine at Morehouse School of Medicine. Yet if I did not get this visa, I would be deported to Nigeria and forced to leave my husband and two daughters behind.

In the months leading up to this day, I had worked intermittently, as the law allowed, and worried interminably. Over the years, my legal status in the country was continually in jeopardy as I attempted to successfully navigate my way from a six-year working visa through to a green card.

It was an exhausting process. I was tempted to give up many times. One time, my husband and my mother urged me to attend our church's monthly "Miracle Service." This service was one of praise and worship, filled with testimonies of God's miraculous working. Yet I did not want to go. My mind was whirling with strategies for how to get myself out of my predicament. Instead of praying in faith, I was nagging God to work everything out for me.

In the end, I went to the service, but I was preoccupied with worry the entire time. The service was almost over when a visiting speaker said she had a word of prophecy for a person in the congregation. I was sometimes skeptical about these revelations, because they always seemed too general to be a convincing word from God for any particular individual. But tonight was different.

"Someone here tonight is giving up on her immigration status," the minister declared. "This person needs to hold on to God and not give up hope. She needs to stand strong until the end."

I was shocked to my bones to hear this. In medical school, we learn that a combination of hypothermia and shock can sometimes cause people to experience something like an out-of-body experience. This was exactly how I felt. Armed with this word of grace, I rose up with fresh energy for my pursuit.

Eventually, I did secure a job. And, although I was denied a labor certificate, I was granted approval for an extension of my working visa. The catch was that the approval depended on getting an approval from the embassy in Lagos. I had to return to Nigeria after all.

The day of my interview dawned. I arrived at the American Embassy at 6 A.M. to find a line snaking for two miles from the entrance to the Atlantic Ocean. I waited in line with my mother, watching the waves beat against the sea wall. The water was beautiful, but the relentless beating of the waves only increased my anxiety.

After three hours, the doors opened and the line started moving. I finally made it into the building and was searched three times, along with every other terrified applicant in line. It took another hour and a half to reach the front desk. I explained what I was there for, and that the paperwork for approval had been forwarded from the United States. The clerk looked at me and shook her head.

"No, honey, there's nothing here," she said. Still, she motioned for me to take a seat.

The interview room was staffed by employees in separate booths. We could clearly hear interactions between the interviewers and applicants. The interviewer in the first booth, a woman, was loud and brutal. I heard her strident voice from the moment I came into the room. I watched as a nervous, middle-aged applicant at her booth became confused about the day and month of her birth.

"Are you trying to lie to me?" the interviewer shouted at the trembling woman. "Do you think I am joking here?"

This interviewer denied visas to almost everyone who faced her. Silently, I sent up a prayer: *Lord, please keep me from being interviewed by this intimidating lady. Please let me be interviewed with dignity.*

When it was finally my turn, I saw that two booths were opening up. One was staffed by a man who seemed gentle in demeanor and whose voice I hadn't heard raised in anger or irritation. The other one was the woman I feared. *Not her, Lord*, I prayed, *please not her.*

Both interviews ended at exactly the same time. I held my breath, praying for the gentleman in the second booth to call me. But the woman beat him to it.

"Next . . . " she began to say, when a staff member interrupted her with a question.

"Next," said the gentleman.

Relieved but nervous, I sat down and waited for the man to look up and speak.

"What is your purpose for coming to Nigeria?" he asked, finally.

This was the question I had hoped not to have to tackle. The answer was complicated, and I didn't know where to begin. My mouth felt dry and empty. I longed for a drink of water. I struggled for words and prayed for courage.

"My working visa expired," I answered. That was the simple truth.

He mumbled some kind of answer.

I handed him copies of the documents I had brought with me. He took them from me and was silent for what seemed like forever. The entire time, I was praying, *Lord, have mercy*.

He asked a few more questions, and then he wrote something in my passport and began gathering up my documents. Then he picked up a green ticket and stamped it with a visa number.

Praise God—I had been approved!

Now, I could return to my family and to my work. My goodness, I was ready to rock the town! We celebrated that night with hot bread and suya—a spiced beef—and I didn't even think about the calories.

Some months later, back home in the United States, I received my approved labor certification. I had written to President Obama about my need, and although my husband and I joke about it, my letter may have had something to do with it. I was on my way to my green card at last!

Our God is never late. He is the God of the last minute, and nothing is impossible for him. God doesn't give us a timeline telling us when his response will come, but of course we humans have one. We want the response by FedEx or UPS the next day, but God doesn't work this way. Why? I guess the reasons are best known to God. But, daily, I am learning through it all, loving my God more and trusting him through my challenges.

Dr. Dolapo Babalola is a practicing family physician in clinical and academic medicine at the Department of Family Medicine for Morehouse School of Medicine in Atlanta, Georgia, where she lives with her family. Born in Lagos, Nigeria, she is a graduate of the University of Guyana Medical School, and she completed her residency at Morehouse. She has written a book about her immigration experience titled My God Even in the Last Minute *(CreateSpace, 2010), from which "God's Perfect Timing" is excerpted and adapted with permission.*

30

What a Smile Hides

MALIN FRIESS, DMD

GENERAL DENTISTRY

KIJABE, KENYA

Here at Kijabe Hospital, our dental staff starts the day with a time of devotions and prayer. Every day, I ask someone to give their testimony of God's grace. We number about 20 people, so I thought this would be a good way for us to get to know each other better.

Kenyans are very different in temperament than Americans. They can be quite reserved and reluctant to stand out in any way. So, the concept of giving a testimony isn't as well known as it is here among Christians in the United States. I often had to encourage people to speak—I went so far as to ask people to put their names on a sign-up sheet!

One of the very last employees to speak was Makena, a woman in her late 20s. Makena was small in stature, not even five feet tall, and a hundred pounds at most. She was our denture lab technician.

Makena had worked in the lab for 12 years, commuting an hour each way on crowded public vans called *matatus*. She had never missed a day of work, and she was never late. She was good with people, very professional, and always patient, especially with our elderly patients.

Makena always seemed to be happy. She hummed while she worked. Her eyes shone behind her large glasses, and she had a wide, beautiful smile with perfectly white teeth. Leave it to a dentist to notice that!

Day after day, Makena took impressions that helped transform toothless, puckered grins into white, full, healthy smiles. Teeth are so much more than something that allows us to chew a drumstick. With the ability to smile again, patients found the confidence to preach in public, to ask someone out on a date, to apply for a job that was previously out of reach. Through a new smile they found joy. So, in a very literal sense, Makena's smile was contagious.

Although Makena was shy, she loved to sing. She had a melodious voice, and she led the worship at her church. At an African church, that's quite a central role—worshippers echo the worship leader as they dance and clap and sing. She readily led the entire hospital staff in worship once a year, when it was the dental staff's turn. She seemed comfortable, almost a different person, in the act of praising God.

But now, in front of the circle of her co-workers in the chai room, Makena was shy. Hiding her mouth behind her Bible, she reluctantly began.

"My childhood is full of memories. Some are good, some are bad," she said.

"I am the seventh of ten children in my family. My mom loved us so much. My dad . . . ," she said, trailing off as tears came into her eyes. "I don't know if I can continue . . .

"My dad was a drunkard. He beat us kids and my mom when he came home at night. He was a politician in our area. The other men did the same thing to their families. They had a lot of power, and no one tried to stop them.

"I had no joy, no ambitions. I was a bad girl; I stole what I wanted from the store. I said I would never marry, that I never would let a man do that to me again.

"But after coming to Kijabe, I met people who cared, people who prayed. In our devotions, I met God, and he transformed me," she continued. "I began to sing again like I always loved to do.

"I met a Christian man, and he truly loves me. We are best friends and we can share anything. We pray together. We got married, and now we have two children that we love so much.

"I am blessed to work at Kijabe Hospital, because here people have a genuine heart. Here, they care about each other," she said.

And then Makena closed with words of faith, powerful words that stay with me even today:

"I believe you do pay for your sins," she said slowly. "My dad is still a drunkard, along with three of my brothers. The alcohol has destroyed his liver, and now he has only a few months to live.

"But God has given me the strength to forgive him. God is everything to me. He is my comfort, my security, my joy. I believe he can transform my father's life just as he transformed mine.

"I am lifted up by God's promises in Psalm 138:

> Though I walk in the midst of trouble, you preserve my life;
> you stretch out your hand against the anger of my foes,
> with your right hand you save me.

The LORD will fulfill his purpose for me;
your love, O LORD, endures forever."

You never really know what is behind a person's smile. A smile can hide a world of pain, but it can also be the joyful sign of a life transformed by God. I learned this from Makena. I praise God for his work in her life.

Dr. Malin Friess is currently practicing dentistry in Albuquerque among the underserved populations of New Mexico. For two years, he worked at Kijabe Hospital in Kenya with Samaritan's Purse and World Medical Mission, where his wife, Sara Cichowski, MD, was a practicing ob/gyn doctor. The couple has three children, Amelia, Meredith, and Oliver.

31

AS THE FLOWERS KNELT

SARA CICHOWSKI, MD

OBSTETRICS AND GYNECOLOGY

KIJABE, KENYA

Trust in the Lord with all your heart
and lean not on your own understanding;
in all your ways submit to him, and he will direct your paths.

PROVERBS 3:5–6

I've been uncertain about publicly airing my sorrow, our sorrow. But as the sorrow expands, it seems dishonest not to incorporate it into this journal of our time here in Kenya with Samaritan's Purse.

It's exhausting trying to hide this heartache as I cope with the demands of mothering, mission work, and treating the challenging and complex conditions of my patients. I also hesitate because I'll be publicly admitting that my husband and I want another child. And that may start people wondering, asking us why it hasn't happened, forcing me into conversations I don't want to have.

The truth is, there is no good explanation for why I've lost three pregnancies here in the past year. No satisfying reason that I can't seem to hold a pregnancy past eight weeks. No comforting explanation for having had three D&Cs at our hospital here, and certainly no understanding as to why this has happened.

Moreover, I'm not sure that being a doctor who knows all the ins and outs of pregnancy, conception, and fertility has helped me. It definitely doesn't help to be surrounded all day by pregnant women, some who don't want to be pregnant, some who shouldn't be pregnant, and some who have tried to end their pregnancies. Even the presence of women women who, like me, have had recurrent pregnancy loss is of no comfort.

The third loss occurred on February 3rd, just days before I turned 32. I was crushed. Why did the heartbeat stop again? I signed the consent for a third dilation and curettage, dreading waking up afterwards, forced to admit that another pregnancy is over. Anxious about being so vulnerably exposed, I wanted to hide from the staff I normally enjoyed seeing and working with.

In Kenya, they call the D&C procedure "cleaning out the uterus," but I know I will not feel clean afterwards, just empty and raw. It's exhausting trying to fill that emptiness and to accept, again, what has happened. And nowhere on the consent form do I give permission for the ache and grief that goes on far longer than the bleeding.

The anesthetist, my friend Mary, prays before the surgery. She says something about God's sovereignty. I cringe when I hear that, and cry, hoping that there really is a plan and purpose to all this.

After my three losses, I found it hard to even walk into the hospital. Before, the hospital had been a a place I loved, a place I inhabited with enthusiasm, where I found fulfillment in helping others heal and in delivering new life. Now, though, this beloved place just makes me feel entombed with grief.

In an effort to find some peace, I began to read *Praying our Goodbyes*, by Joyce Rupp. In it, she includes Robert Frost's poem, "Lodged." Frost writes about a storm lashing a garden so severely that "the flowers actually knelt / and lay lodged—though not dead."

I could say with the poet: "I know how the flowers felt."

At the time, I thought that I couldn't feel any lower, or at least that God wouldn't allow any more suffering. I thought that I was bent enough from the pain and therefore would not have to endure more. I was wrong.

Over the summer, while vacationing with family in a remote part of Oregon, I awoke with pain and bleeding. In my heart, I knew what was happening, but still I hoped that I was wrong. After all, just a few days before, I had seen a specialist who had said everything was fine with this pregnancy.

We rushed to the nearest town—90 long minutes away—and as the ultrasound technician scanned my abdomen, I saw the unmistakable signs of a ruptured ectopic pregnancy. Another loss. I could hardly breathe from the pain and the shock.

So, again, I sign a consent form. This time the procedure is listed as "exploratory laparoscopy with removal of ectopic pregnancy." The complications are listed as well: bleeding, infection, injury to other organs. Where can I sign saying that I've had enough? That the organ most injured isn't my uterus or my fallopian tubes but my heart. That I don't think it can bear any more grief.

I want to scream, "This isn't fair!" Instead, I ask for medicine to help me sleep and induce a temporary amnesia before surgery. I don't like thinking about what will happen once I am wheeled into the operating room, because I know the exact steps of the procedure.

I know the instruments by heart and how to use them. Normally I see them as tools for healing, as a means to stop bleeding and save a life. But now I loathe them for the pain I perceive them as causing. After all, as I try so hard not to blame God, isn't it easier to blame the instruments?

Suffering is a part of life, I've found. Most of us have at times felt so burdened that we literally feel crushed physically, emotionally, and spiritually, as I do now. Yet being forced to my knees as Frost's flowers were, shoved there by my sorrow, reminds me of prayer. I think the flowers—and I—have assumed the correct position. In my pain, kneeling acknowledges the humility I must have before a sovereign God. Being on my knees in prayer before the Lord changes me, gives me a certain power. I trust with the psalmist that "The Lord helps the fallen and lifts those bent beneath their loads" (Psalm 145:14 NLT).

My understanding of why this sorrow has befallen us, and why it has befallen us here in Kenya where we are confronted daily with so much suffering, is limited. And I will not find peace if I continue to ask, "Why, Lord? Why me?" Instead, I will try to pray, "What is next, Lord? Be near me, Lord. Please, will you enable me to keep working here? Please, Lord, strengthen me for my children and husband. Comfort me." Yes, I am kneeling, but I am merely lodged, and not dead.

Dr. Sara Cichowski served for two years at Kijabe Hospital, Kenya, with Samaritan's Purse and World Medical Mission, along with her husband, Malin Friess, DMD. She completed a three-year fellowship in

pelvic reconstruction at the University of New Mexico and is currently
an assistant professor at the University of New Mexico and Veteran's
Health Administration Hospital. The couple have three children, Amelia,
Meredith, and Oliver.

Robert Frost's poem "Lodged" first appeared in *West-Running Brook* (New York: Henry Holt, 1928).

32

EMERGENCY IN FLIGHT

VISHAL PAREKH, MD, FACP

INTERNAL MEDICINE

ATLANTA, GEORGIA

While I was a resident at St. Barnabas Hospital in New York, I took a flight home on Delta Air Lines to visit my family in Mumbai.

I had just come off a month's rotation in the emergency room, and I was exhausted. I was looking forward to putting my feet up and enjoying my vacation. It was a nighttime flight, so after the dinner service, I closed my eyes and quickly fell asleep.

Sometime in the middle of the night, around one or two o'clock in the morning, the pilot made an announcement asking for any physicians on board to come forward and identify themselves. I must have been sleeping lightly, because I heard the announcement and got up to offer my help.

I was met in the aisle by a flight attendant who said that an elderly gentleman at the front of the coach section was feeling unwell.

Earl was sitting in an aisle seat, with his wife to his right. When I got to him, he was sweating, his head was pitched backward, and he was gasping for air. He would open his eyes for a few seconds, but then they would close and roll back in his head. He was not able to talk or orient himself. His wife said he had been unresponsive for several minutes.

Given his symptoms, Earl could be experiencing several things—I guessed a stroke, a heart attack, or a hypoglycemic episode. His wife said he was diabetic, so low blood sugar would make sense. She said he had taken his insulin before he ate dinner, but that he hadn't eaten much. She also said he had a history of high blood pressure, although he had not had any incidents related to it in the past.

Upon hearing these two pieces of information, my fear was that Earl was experiencing two medical emergencies at once, something to do with his heart on top of a low blood sugar episode. I was pretty sure that I would have no means of dealing with a heart attack or a stroke.

I asked the flight attendant to bring me a blood pressure cuff. Fortunately, the plane had one. Earl's heart rate and his pulse were fine—no unexpected numbers there. On top of that, I was relieved to see that he wasn't experiencing any paralysis, nor had he stopped moving his hands or legs, which would have been a sign of an ongoing stroke.

I asked the flight attendant to bring me a glucometer, so I could check Earl's blood sugar. She handed me one, but it didn't seem to be working. I tried several times to get a reading, but could not.

With nothing more to go on, I decided to treat Earl's symptoms as a hypoglycemic attack. I would try to revive him by getting him to drink juice, which would raise his blood sugar quickly. I figured I could at least revive him enough so that we had time to make an emergency landing and get him to a hospital.

It isn't easy to get diabetic people to eat or drink when they are slipping into a diabetic coma. After the blood sugar has fallen below a certain point, they will resist your efforts to help them. Earl was well beyond resisting—he was barely responsive enough to ingest anything. I kept shouting his name and shaking him gently by the shoulders. Although lethargic, he was responding minimally to my voice, and I was able to get him to take a few sips.

In this way, I was gradually able to get him to drink three or four glasses of juice. But suddenly, he vomited violently, losing a good deal of the juice. He was still responding, though, so I continued to feed him sips of juice.

While all this was going on, the pilot asked me to alert him if he should plan for an emergency landing. I told the flight attendant that if I did not see improvement soon, the pilot should definitely plan to land. We held off, though, while I continued to feed Earl sips of juice.

After about seven or eight glasses, Earl gradually began to breathe better, and he became more responsive, although he was still drowsy. I could feel his body relax, and his sweating abated. He recognized his wife, and he could tell us where he was. I checked his blood pressure and pulse again, and all his numbers were fine.

My diagnosis was correct—I had done the right thing.

The crisis lasted about a half an hour. Once Earl was able to stand, the flight attendant moved us into first-class seats, so I could keep an eye on him. I was connected by phone with Delta's 24-hour medical team and spoke with a physician about the incident.

I sat with Earl for a few hours, chatting with him and observing him. He was an economist, he said, and he and his wife were on their way to a family function. They were scheduled to change planes in Paris, where our flight was headed.

From my observations, I felt that Earl was improving and the pilot didn't need to make an emergency landing, so we continued on to

Paris. After a few hours, Earl returned to his wife and I went back to my seat. The couple thanked me profusely for my help—Earl's wife even took a photo of me with her husband.

Strange as it may sound, this is a wonderful memory for me. Even now, I am totally in awe when I think of this incident. It remains the most inspiring event of my medical career. I had never before encountered an emergency outside of a clinical setting. For the first time, I felt that my education and my service had really helped someone when nothing else would have. And it was only by the grace of God that I was able to help.

On top of that, I enjoyed the first-class seat that Delta offered me for the rest of my flight!

Dr. Vishal Parekh is assistant professor of clinical medicine for the Department of Internal Medicine at Morehouse School of Medicine in Atlanta, Georgia. He is a Fellow in the American College of Physicians. He has a special interest in issues surrounding hypertension, diabetes, and lipids. He and his wife, Binita, live in Atlanta, Georgia.

33

A MIRACLE BABY

RACHEL MCLAUGHLIN, MD

OBSTETRICS AND GYNECOLOGY

BOMET, KENYA

Last week I was on call at the hospital, performing a C-section with one of my interns in the early evening. The mom was pregnant with twins—her eighth and ninth children—both in the breech position. But other than some increased bleeding from the uterine incision that we were working to control, things were going fine.

At that moment, a nurse poked her head into the operating room and called out to the team, "C-section for cord prolapse coming down the hallway!"

Cord prolapse is an emergency situation. An unborn baby's total oxygen supply comes from the umbilical cord, which is attached to the mother through the placenta. Usually, when a woman's water breaks, the baby's head pushes against the open cervix, acting as a cork or barrier so that the umbilical cord stays inside the uterus.

Once in a while, although it's a rare occurrence, a loop of cord will slide past the baby's head through the cervix. The baby's head then compresses the cord against the cervix or vaginal wall, cutting off blood flow and oxygen to the baby. The baby needs to be delivered via

C-section immediately to prevent severe brain damage or death due to hypoxia, a lack of oxygen.

In this kind of emergency, immediately means operating within five to ten minutes.

I left my intern to finish up the C-section, which was going well and was almost complete, and ran to the other operating room. The only history I had on the patient was that she had just arrived at the hospital with the umbilical cord already hanging out, and that she was close to her due date.

I did a quick exam to feel the cord. It was still pulsating with the baby's heartbeat—that was a good sign—although it was on the slow side.

We put the mother to sleep, and I started the C-section. When I opened the uterus, I found that instead of being head down or breech, the baby was lying sideways in the uterus. It was difficult to maneuver the baby out of the uterus, but as soon as it was delivered, the baby started crying. A beautiful, healthy baby boy!

Sitting in the operating room after the surgery waiting for my patient to awaken from the anesthesia, I looked through the paperwork that came in with her and found a note from the referring clinic. It said she had come in to the clinic at 3 P.M. and had been diagnosed with the cord prolapse at that time.

At 3 P.M.! I started her surgery at the hospital at 8 P.M.—five hours later!

That was an incredible lapse of time. Reflecting on why this baby hadn't died—as the vast majority of babies in this situation do in Kenya—I think it was his malpresentation that saved him. Because he was lying sideways, the cord wasn't being compressed by his head, his feet, or his bottom.

But let me change that statement. With all the odds stacked against him, I think a miracle saved this little boy. Events like this are why I went into obstetrics. Praise God!

Dr. Rachel McLaughlin is a practicing ob/gyn physician living in Bomet, Kenya, and working at Tenwek Hospital with Samaritan's Purse. She and her husband, Eric, a family practitioner at Tenwek, are planning to serve with World Harvest Mission in the African country of Burundi. The couple has two children, Maggie and Ben. "A Miracle Baby" *is adapted with permission from the couple's blog,* The Adventures of Eric and Rachel *(www.doctorsmclaughlin.blogsspot.com).*

34

You Look Like Jesus

Eric McLaughlin, MD

Family Medicine

Bomet, Kenya

I was walking to the sink in Tenwek Hospital's neonatal intensive care unit for about the thirtieth time one day to wash my hands. Two nurses stood nearby filling syringes with medicines. They were speaking in Kipsigis, the local language in this part of Kenya, of which I know about five words.

One of the nurses said something that ended in a word that sounded like "Jesus." Intuitively, I turned to them.

"What did she say?" I asked the other nurse, who spoke English.

"What?" the nurse answered, deflecting me innocently.

"What did she just say?" I asked again.

There was a long pause while the two nurses glanced at each other.

"She said you look like Jesus," the nurse finally said, both of them giggling.

It was not the first time I'd heard this since moving to Kenya. In fact, I've heard it many times over.

I don't think I look Jewish, so I really don't think I could look like Jesus. No one here has met any Jewish people, though, except for the Messianic Jewish dermatologist who came to visit earlier this year.

But everyone here has seen the "Jesus" film, and they think I look a lot like Brian Deacon, the guy who plays Jesus in the movie. I'm white and I have a beard. I guess that's close enough.

I figured out the movie connection early on.

One day soon after I arrived here, I went to the pharmacy to see if we had a saline nasal spray. (We had one. I prescribed it. Then we had none.) The Kenyan pharmacy tech said to me, "You know, you look Jewish. I have a video with Jesus in it, and every time I see you, I think you look like him."

Not two hours later, I headed to the nursery, and the nurse asked, "Are you Jewish?"

"You're saying that because I look like Jesus in the movie, right?" I asked.

The nurse smiled, just a bit self-conscious.

"Yes," she answered sheepishly.

This morning again, the nurse from the neonatal intensive care unit greeted me with, "Hello, Jesus." This time I called her on it.

"Why do you think I look like Jesus?" I asked her.

"Well, you are a Christian, and you are Christ-like, so I call you Jesus," she answered, lamely trying to pretend that it wasn't my beard and my whiteness.

I gestured to a Kenyan friend nearby.

"Enoch is a Christian and he's Christ-like, but you're not calling him Jesus," I goaded her.

I guess this comparison is just one of the odd things about being in a white minority here. Children are forever waving to you from the roadside. Today on my rounds, I caught a patient out of the corner of my eye taking a picture of me with his cell phone.

A veteran missionary once jokingly advised me, "You're always the bride at the wedding!"

This unsolicited attention seems novel at first, but, to be honest, it can feel oppressive when you are actually living somewhere overseas for a long period of time.

Truth be told, though, I actually got this comparison before I even arrived in Kenya. When I was working in a clinic in Ypsilanti, Michigan, I treated many Latino patients, for whom my friend Jenny, a medical student, would translate. After an appointment with a familiar patient one day, Jenny and I left the exam room together. She broke into a wide smile.

"When you left the exam room for a minute," she said, "the patient turned to me and said, 'You know, I feel like I've gotten to know you, so I'll share something with you.

"'I think my doctor looks like Jesus,'" he confided. "'So when he came into the room, I thought, *The Lord is my doctor and he has come to heal me!*'"

There are worse things in this world than being mistaken for Jesus. Lord Jesus, we are all being transformed into your image.

Dr. Eric McLaughlin practices family medicine at Tenwek Hospital in Bomet, Kenya. He and his wife, Rachel, an ob/gyn doctor at the hospital, are planning to serve with World Harvest Mission in Burundi. The couple has two children, Maggie and Ben. "You Look Like Jesus" is adapted with permission from the blog, The Adventures of Eric and Rachel. *The McLaughlins serve with a team of friends—all doctors and their families in the two-year post-residency program of* Samaritan's Purse—*who serve together in Kenya. The team's blog* Word and Deed *can be found at mccropders.com.*

35

IT'S PROBABLY NOTHING

EDWIN LEAP, MD

EMERGENCY MEDICINE

SENECA, SOUTH CAROLINA

*Praise be to the God and Father of our Lord Jesus Christ, the Father
of compassion and the God of all comfort, who comforts us in all
our troubles, so that we can comfort those in any trouble with the
comfort we ourselves have received from God.*

2 CORINTHIANS 1:3–4

I met my wife at a Halloween party in college when we were 19 years
old. Jan was a blue-eyed, black-haired beauty, with legs that could
make a guy weep. She was dressed as a mime. I was dressed as a
doctor. No surprise there—I was a big pre-med nerd!

A few months later, a group of us went sledding, and a fire began
to flicker between us. It wasn't long before we went on our first date,
and many more followed.

We were poor, skinny, college kids who loved to laugh and eat
cheap pizza. We went to free movies on campus and met up between
classes. I still can see her, tripping across the grass in a red hat and

cape, coming to meet me. She was beautiful then and she remains so to me now.

Time passed, as it does for every couple. We'd been married for 20 years, and known each other for 27 years, when Jan began to complain of a swollen lymph node on the left side of her neck.

"It's probably nothing," we told ourselves. It was autumn, and we'd all had colds, sore throats, and fevers. A tender, swollen lymph node didn't raise any alarms.

But, in November, the swelling was more painful than ever. Still, we told ourselves it was nothing—probably nothing, right?—but it was time to see the ear, nose, and throat doctor.

"Probably nothing," the doctor said. But he was a cautious, competent surgeon, so he said it should be evaluated. A CT scan showed an enlarged node, but nothing else, no other adenopathy. We figured, "It's probably nothing."

That was in essence what the pathologist said when he did the fine-needle aspirate. "Some squamous cells. They don't look malignant," he said. "Can't say it's cancer, can't say it isn't. But it needs to be taken out."

The pathology report read, "Squamous cells with cystic changes, consistent with branchial cleft cyst." I liked that. It meant it was probably nothing.

The day Jan was scheduled for surgery, her surgeon blocked out four hours, just in case. "I doubt we'll need it," he said, "but if we find anything, we'll need to explore." Another way of saying "probably nothing," I convinced myself.

But just an hour into the surgery, our "probably nothing" collapsed suddenly into "definitely something." The doctor called me from the operating room.

"Ed, I talked to the pathologist," he said. "It's metastatic squamous cell cancer. We'll need to remove all the lymph nodes in a modified radical neck dissection." Cancer!

At that moment, all of my composure, all of my medical knowledge and skill, and all of my years of experience dissolved. I simply and utterly fell to pieces. My beautiful bride, my partner in life, had cancer. I ceased to be a physician, and I became nothing more than a terrified husband, a horrified father. I cried like I hadn't cried in years.

Seven hours passed. We had plenty of support—dear friends, my partner in practice, my emergency room family, and my pastor all came to my side. Our entire Sunday School class began to pray for us, even before Jan emerged from the OR.

When I next saw my dear wife, two large incisions graced her lovely neck, and two long drains drew off the bloody fluid resulting from the surgery. She was sweating and confused. "That was fast," she said with a weak smile. "Not really," I said.

As she came out of the anesthesia and became more aware, I had to tell her the news. "I have cancer?" she asked.

Still, we were ignorant. We had no idea what all this meant. We simply kept falling down the rabbit hole. My thoughts were like a runaway train, headed for a washed-out bridge. All I could see was darkness and fear.

I spent every evening sleeping by the fire, as close to Jan as possible. I wanted to do nothing but watch movies with her, to eat and to sleep. My children, accustomed to a fairly unshakeable Papa, saw me begin to unravel. I did my best not to frighten them, so when I needed to scream and cry, I screamed and cried in my truck, alone.

At work, I was constantly filled with anxiety, anxiety that began as soon as I walked in the door and logged onto the computer. Every patient I saw represented my wife. Every tragedy ignited my fear. Everyone with cancer was a metaphor for her.

But my wife is a ball of courage. The day after the surgery she was home—in pain, but in good spirits. "I don't have time for this. I have children to raise!" she told me.

Jan's course of treatment for oropharyngeal cancer was brutal—three months of chemotherapy along with 35 doses of radiation. She was exhausted. She was so tired of vomiting. Her tongue became swollen and ulcerated, which made the vomiting hurt even more.

Jan ate so little for so long that even nutrition given through a feeding tube nauseated her, starting the cycle of vomiting all over. I gave her IV fluids and nausea medicine, but still the vomiting went on and on.

Her struggles didn't end with the chemo. Two or three weeks after her last chemo, she suffered a pulmonary embolus, a blockage in an artery of the lungs. We rushed her to the hospital—I don't like to think how close we came to losing her. Yet she defied all medical expectations and came home from the hospital two days later.

I cherish my wife; a threat to her is like a threat to my own life. We are one, and that's how it feels when half of you is in danger. I will never, ever view my patients' fears and vulnerabilities in the same way again. I have learned compassion and empathy as I never knew it before.

In this time, we have leaned as never before on God, on family, on our church family, on friends, and on one another. We are very independent Appalachians. Leaning isn't easy, but we are learning.

It has been an intense time, filled with pain, discomfort, and fear. But also, surprisingly, a time of love, hope, and delight. We have learned, as never before, what the vows "in sickness and in health" mean. We have discovered that intimacy and passion change form during times like this. Holding hands in the midst of fever and weakness is strangely romantic, and praying out loud for the one you love is more passionate than the most contrived sonnet.

As I write this, Jan is thriving—six months from her diagnosis, three months from her last chemotherapy and radiation treatment, and almost three months from her life-threatening pulmonary embolus. Her prognosis is good. She has traveled to visit family and friends, she has gone to her gym, she has even taught Vacation Bible School.

Rationally, I know that it is likely she will have no problem and no residual malignancy. She was treated as aggressively as possible. Still, I drive her to distraction with the question, "How are you feeling?" I pester her endlessly to eat. I imagine every bump or cough a metastasis. I have envisioned all the worst outcomes imaginable. And yet, God has seen us through so much.

I have always loved going on dates with my darling Jan—ever since those long-ago dates in college—and our time together is even more precious to me now as she recovers. If she asks me, out of the blue, "Do you want to go out tonight?" my instant response is, "Yes!" And when she holds my hand, I grip it for all I'm worth.

Sickness is misery. Cancer is horrifying. But in every difficulty lies a gift. And if this one bonds our marriage more tightly than ever, then it was not empty suffering. And if it reminds us that we are loved by our Maker, our Redeemer, in the same powerful, changeless, unmitigated way, then perhaps it was a blessing after all.

Dr. Edwin Leap practices emergency medicine with Blue Ridge Emergency Physicians in Seneca, South Carolina. He and his wife, Jan, have four children, Sam, Seth, Elijah, and Elysa. Dr. Leap writes regularly for The Greenville *(South Carolina)* News, Emergency Medicine News, *and* The Baptist Courier. *He has published three books through Booklocker:* Working Knights *(2004),* Cats Don't Hike *(2006), and* The Practice Test *(2010). "It's Probably Nothing" is adapted with permission from multiple posts from Dr. Leap's blog edwinleap.com. A version of his story was also published as "It's Probably Nothing" in* Emergency Medicine News *(Second Opinion column, February 2011).*

36

SPARKS OF LIGHT

WILLIAM T. GRIFFIN, DDS

GENERAL DENTISTRY

NEWPORT NEWS, VIRGINIA

Crystal came into my dental office one day with a huge smile on her face and radiating an aura of peace. I couldn't believe this was the same unhappy young woman I had seen just a few months earlier.

I first began seeing Crystal when she was 16 years old. A high decay rate made her a regular visitor to my practice. In recent years, some of her cavities had crept dangerously close to the nerves in her teeth, causing sensitivity and eventually necessitating two root canals.

During her last few visits, Crystal had requested prescription medications to help her deal with the pain.

When a patient requests pain medicine, it can create a dilemma for a doctor. While we want to be compassionate and ease a person's pain, we also don't want to contribute to a dependence on mind-altering medications. Often I wonder whether prescription medicine is really needed, but I almost always give the patient the benefit of the doubt.

In Crystal's case, though, I strongly suspected her desire for pain medicine had nothing to do with her dental problems. That being the case, I thought the most loving thing I could do was to deny her request. I sent her a letter explaining my rationale for not writing the prescription she claimed to need. I also said I would not be able to continue as her dentist unless she allowed me to treat the source of her alleged pain.

This was a hard letter for me to write. I knew that Crystal had lived a difficult life, with more than her share of heartaches. During her nine years as my patient, the Lord had given me several opportunities to share his love with her. I was afraid my letter might sever our fragile doctor-patient relationship altogether.

It was four months after sending this letter that Crystal walked into my office looking like an entirely new person. Cautiously, I asked her about the prescriptions, and Crystal admitted she had tried to deceive me.

"The prescriptions were to get high on," she said. "My husband and I had just separated, and I didn't want to deal with my issues and problems at the time.

"Alcohol was my main addiction, but I used anything that could get me high, because it was an escape. In my head I was saying, 'I'm feeling pain, and I don't want to feel pain.' But I was exaggerating the pain because I was addicted."

I asked Crystal about my letter denying her the prescriptions.

"It hurt," she said. "It hurt a lot because I knew then that my drug problem was becoming obvious. My family knew about it, but now my dentist was seeing it, and he was acknowledging it, which hit hard."

Even so, Crystal hadn't yet hit bottom. It took even more devastating events to bring her to that place.

"Unfortunately, it took me sitting in a jail cell to realize that I no longer could control my life," she said. "Because of my addiction, my marriage failed, I lost my home, and I lost my son.

"My grandmother—the wonderful woman who raised me and who had loved me unconditionally—didn't want me in her house any more because she couldn't trust me.

"Everything around me was falling apart," she said. "It took a spiral to the bottom of the hole to finally realize that I had no control. Sitting in that jail cell, I knew that it was time to allow Jesus to take control of my life."

Crystal said she'd had an upbringing in a church that preached the gospel, but she said her visits to my office got her attention in a way that nothing else had.

"When I came in here, I wanted what you and the nurses had," she said. "You and your staff had a spark, a light that shined through to me. The love of God was in the whole office. I knew this was more than a dental office. You really cared about showing the love of God, and that meant a lot to me."

I have done some deep fillings on Crystal since that day, and, by the grace of God, she hasn't needed any pain medication. "The Lord explained to me I didn't need any mind-altering substances," she has told me.

Through Crystal, I have found the confidence to give patients what they need, not necessarily what they ask for. As doctors, we have a responsibility to use our professional knowledge for the betterment of our patients. Our role is to be faithful, to show the love of Christ to every patient, and pray that the Lord will use the efforts of his people to change hearts.

Dr. William T. Griffin practices general dentistry in Newport News, Virginia. Dr. Griffin serves as dental director and president of the board of the Lackey Free Medical-Dental Clinic in Yorktown, Virginia, and goes on two to three dental mission trips each year. "Sparks of Light" was written as "Interview of a Patient" and adapted with permission from Today's Christian Doctor *(Spring, 2010), a publication of the Christian Medical and Dental Society. He and his wife, Linda, have two children, Katie and Will.*

37

No Fear for the Future

Robert Orr, MD, CM

Medical Ethics and Bioethics

Loma Linda, California

Betty was a long-time patient at my family practice in Vermont. I had cared for her husband one night in the emergency room after his heart had stopped while the couple was enjoying an evening of square dancing. Sadly, we were not able to resuscitate him.

A few weeks after his death, I had Betty come to my office to talk about how she was doing and how she was coping with her grief. From then on, she became my patient. For five or six years I helped her manage her diabetes and hypertension. She became dear to our family—we had her over for Christmas dinner one year, and she made us a beautiful afghan that we treasured.

Now Betty was in her 80s, and one day she came to my office to be checked for some vaginal bleeding. Through the years, I had urged her to have annual Pap smears, but she had declined, believing she was too old to need the tests.

I found that Betty had an advanced uterine cancer. It had already spread as far as her lungs. Nevertheless, she had surgery and did well for quite a while.

Eventually, though, Betty became chronically short of breath. We discovered through X-rays that the cancer had metastasized in the periphery of her lungs. Fluid was building up between her lungs and the chest wall.

I managed this complication by having Betty come to the emergency room once a week to draw off the fluid with a needle. One week I would do one side, the next week, the other side.

Even so, Betty became increasingly frail. I began to make house calls to check on her. We talked about our faith—she was a devout Catholic—and on many occasions, we prayed together. I believe we may have even sung a hymn or two!

One time she arrived at the emergency room for the chest tap. She was extremely short of breath on this day, struggling for each meager breath.

We helped her sit down on the exam table and settled her feet on a chair beside the table. I gathered up the syringe and needle and prepared to swab her chest. But, suddenly, Betty stopped me. She put up her hand, as if it were a stop sign.

In an effort that was terribly painful for her, she spoke haltingly, one word at a time, gathering her strength for each word.

"You . . . have . . . the . . . power . . . " she said.

I didn't understand what she meant. I asked her a few questions, trying to get at her meaning.

Then, all at once, I understood. *I had the power*, she was saying, *to determine when she died.*

During my house calls, Betty and I had talked about end-of-life decisions. She had clearly stated her wishes. She did not want to end up in the intensive care unit, and she did not want to be kept alive on a ventilator. If it came to that, she said, she wanted just comfort care.

"Are you saying that you don't want me to do the tap?" I asked Betty now. "Is it time to focus on your comfort and not postpone your death any longer?"

"Yes," she answered.

I began to put away my equipment. A nurse and I helped Betty lie back on the table, and we elevated her head to ease her breathing. I took her right hand in mine and began to pray with her.

In my prayer, I thanked God for Betty's life and for the assurance of her eternal life in heaven. I asked God to help me treat her adequately, so that her life would end quickly and she would die in comfort.

The nurse was clearly uncomfortable when I prayed that Betty would die quickly, but there was no question in my mind that I was following my patient's wishes. We admitted Betty to the hospital and began to provide palliative care, including morphine for pain management. Within 36 hours she died, sedated, and in no pain.

Betty's statement made a huge impression on me. From her, I understood that more often than we realize, we can determine the course of our death by the choices we make. I would never actively induce the death of a patient or advocate that anyone do so. But because of the time Betty and I had spent together talking of our faith, I knew Betty was not fearful of her future, that she was looking forward to eternity with God, so I did not hesitate to follow her lead. I have faced this situation with individuals and with their families hundreds of times since then, but none more memorably than this time with Betty.

Dr. Robert Orr is a Senior Fellow with The Center for Bioethics & Human Dignity, where he is also co-chair of the Healthcare Ethics Council. He is Professor of Bioethics at The Graduate College of Union University and at Trinity International University. He also is Professor of Medical Ethics at Loma Linda University and Professor of Family Medicine at the University of Vermont College of Medicine. For 18 years, he had a family practice in Vermont. He has written extensively in the field of medical ethics, including the book Medical Ethics: The Faith Factor *(Wm. B. Eerdmans, 2009). He and his wife, Joyce, have three adult children.*

38

A RISKY PLAN

J. DEANE WALDMAN, MD, MBA

PEDIATRIC CARDIOLOGY

ALBUQUERQUE, NEW MEXICO

Gina, the first child born to young Hispanic parents, had an abnormal heart.

We knew about Gina's heart, because we had seen the problem on an echocardiogram when she was still in the womb. The heart of a fetus develops in a specific step-by-step sequence. Gina's heart had missed a step and critical parts were missing. The defect prevented a normal flow of blood through her heart and lungs. Gina could survive for a while with this condition, but eventually it would kill her.

Until recently, fixing a heart problem like Gina's was not possible. Surgeons had developed some procedures that helped babies like her, but they could not entirely repair the heart. All babies with Gina's type of heart malformation eventually died.

One surgeon I knew had experimented with a surgical repair technique that completely fixed the baby's heart. Dr. Harris wasn't a cowboy surgeon—he didn't do risky procedures for the thrill of it. He had performed the surgery hundreds of times, and his outcomes were better than anyone else's anywhere in the world.

Dr. Harris lived 1,200 miles away. I put in a request to the insurance company to refer Gina to him. He was her best hope. But the insurer refused my request. They said they had a contract with a different surgeon, and that I could only send Gina to him.

I put in a call to the approved doctor. I knew of him—he was also well respected—and he said he could do the surgery "just fine." But then he added that he would use the old surgical method. That didn't sit well with me, as I knew that surgery wasn't as good as Dr. Harris's surgery.

"I've got to find a way to get Gina to Dr. Harris," I insisted to her parents. They were only kids themselves, 19 or 20 years old, and they were frightened.

I called the medical director of the insurance company again. I shared published data with him that proved Dr. Harris was the best surgeon—in fact, the *only* surgeon—for Gina. Any other doctor simply was not acceptable, I said. "Sending her anywhere else would force me to practice bad medicine," I stated. The medical director would not budge.

While I was going back and forth with the insurance company, we were keeping Gina alive with the use of a medicine that allowed blood to flow into her lungs. Without it, she would soon have too little oxygen in her blood and she would die.

This medicine could be given only through a vein. It could not be taken orally. So, Gina remained in the hospital on an IV while we battled the insurance company. I kept up the pressure on them, threatening to take my case public on the nightly news and looking into the possibility of a lawsuit.

Meanwhile, Gina's father had been doing some investigation of his own. He discovered that he could work around the impasse by switching insurance companies. The catch was that the family had to be with the new insurance company for 30 days before coverage could begin. Or, Gina had to be discharged from the hospital.

Gina didn't have 30 days, so that option was out. But discharging her from the hospital was a dangerous route. I would have to stop giving her the protective medicine. She might die before we could get her back into the hospital.

We kept up the barrage of phone calls, letters, and e-mails to the insurance company, but we weren't making any progress. After talking with the head of the neonatal intensive care unit where the baby was being cared for, I decided we had to take our chances and let Gina go home.

The plan was this: We would release Gina late in the day, and then make an appointment for her to see me first thing the next morning. Doctors in the NICU would reserve a bed for her, in case she needed it. We had it all mapped out, yet it was a risky plan.

When word of my decision reached the nursing staff, they reported me to the hospital's risk management department and to the chair of my department. Suddenly, I was on the receiving end of a flurry of irate calls from the hospital's lawyers and the department chairperson.

"What are you doing?" she asked me. "Do you understand the risk that you're exposing our hospital to?"

I understood the risks alright. But we were stuck. As terrible as it was, discharging Gina was our only option.

So, with the approval of the parents, we discharged Gina at 3 P.M. on a Thursday.

At 8 A.M. Friday, the parents were at my office door with Gina in her baby carrier. As expected, Gina had deteriorated overnight. But she was alive. After readmitting her to the hospital, we restarted her medication. Soon, she was in good condition again.

In the brief time that Gina had been home, her father had worked a miracle. I give him all the credit—he was able to switch insurance companies overnight. I put in a call to the medical director of the new insurance company and convinced him that we needed to refer Gina to Dr. Harris.

In the NICU, curtained off from the rest of the unit, I discussed details of the transfer with the neonatal doctor caring for Gina. She commiserated with me about everything I had gone through to get Gina the care she needed.

I didn't know it then, but Gina's mother was on the other side of the curtain, taking in every word of our conversation. Until then, she may not have been aware of the extent of our battle with the insurance company. I had been very circumspect.

Just before the transport team arrived at the hospital, I went back to the NICU to check on the baby. Gina's mother approached me with tears in her eyes. She put her hand on my shoulder.

"Thank you for fighting for my baby," she said, her voice small and shaky.

This is why I get up every morning and head to work. This is why we all fight these battles. Gina is a healthy baby girl today, and I played a role in that. It's a wonderful feeling. It feeds my soul.

Dr. J. Deane Waldman is a pediatric cardiologist at Children's Hospital Heart Center, Children's Hospital of New Mexico, in Albuquerque. He writes about healthcare reform on his blogs, Uproot Healthcare *(www.uproothealthcare.com) and* The System MD *(www.*

thesystemmd.com). He holds a master's degree in business administration and has written two books. Uproot U.S. Healthcare *(Trafford, 2003) examines the U.S. healthcare system as if it were a patient, uncovering the problematic roots of its symptoms in order to arrive at appropriate diagnosis and treatment.* Not Right!—A Prequel to Uproot U.S. Healthcare *(forthcoming) explores the right to health care and asks the question, "What do 'We the Patients' really want?" "A Risky Plan" was adapted with permission from* Not Right! *He and his wife, Mary, have two adult children, Alex and Dana, and two grandchildren, Cole and Eli.*

39

A Husband Comes Home

DANIEL CLAPP, MD

FAMILY MEDICINE

AMHERST, MASSACHUSETTS

After I completed my medical training in the early 1960s, I went as a doctor with a mission organization to the Philippines, where I provided family care for an orphanage and surrounding communities in the Bukidnon province of Mindanao.

To give you an idea of the primitive nature of living conditions there at the time, let me share a question from the public health exam I had to take in order to practice medicine in the Philippines: "Please describe and illustrate four different sanitary methods for human waste disposal." The question obviously referred to outhouse use—a topic that hadn't come up in my American medical school education!

One aspect of public health that was completely ignored in the Philippines was contraception. At the time, it was still illegal even in parts of the United States to prescribe birth control for unmarried women. Its almost nonexistent use by women in the Philippines, married or single, reflected the practice of a Roman Catholic society of the 1960s, although laws have since changed.

Because of the lack of information and resources, women in this area often had ten or twelve pregnancies during their childbearing years. Commonly, two or three children died from malnutrition or starvation, because the family was too poor to feed their children. Many infants died from protein and vitamin deficiencies. Maternal death in childbirth was not unusual.

I learned of a contraceptive research trial being conducted by the Pathfinder Fund in Boston. The organization was founded by Clarence Gamble, the Procter & Gamble heir who supported efforts to make contraception available and affordable for women around the world. The trial called for collecting data from clinics outside of the United States in order to document the effectiveness and safety of the IUD (intrauterine device).

In this trial, the fund provided IUDs to physicians who agreed to conduct diligent follow-up care and report their research statistics. After sending off the required paperwork, I received 100 IUDs in the mail, along with a mimeographed instruction sheet on the proper sterilization technique, insertion, and follow-up care.

That's all I had to go on—it was a case of "read about one, do one"—but it was enough. I began to dispense the IUDs, keeping a log to report on the device's safety and efficacy. My patients had no significant troubles—unlike in the United States years later, where infections almost forced IUDs off the market. Eventually I ended up dispensing and reporting data on 325 IUDs.

One day, a woman came in for a follow-up exam. She had been my seventh patient to receive an IUD.

During the course of the exam, the woman unexpectedly teared up.

"You know, doctor," she said, "I am so thankful to you. Now my husband can come back home to me."

It turned out that this woman and her husband had 13 children. They could not afford to support any more children, so the husband had taken a job on another Philippine island and reluctantly left his family behind. Apparently, this was a standard method of birth control for overwhelmed families.

"Now that I am protected," she said, "we can live together as a family again."

This was a poignant moment for me as a physician. It was immensely satisfying to have such a significant effect on the family life of my patients. God really has created us for good works, and I'm so thankful to have had the opportunity to serve him.

Dr. Daniel Clapp spent seven years as a medical missionary in the Philippines and practiced medicine in Amherst, Massachusetts, for 31 years until his retirement in 2002. For those 31 years, he was coordinator of women's health care for the University of Massachusetts, and for 17 years he was team physician for the athletic department. He has returned to the Philippines over the years, the last time in 2003. He provides free care at four area medical clinics and performs physical exams for recruits at Westover Air Reserve Base in Chicopee, Massachusetts. He and his wife, Solveig, have two children and five grandchildren.

40

THE SMALLEST ONE

JACOB DELAROSA, MD
CARDIOTHORACIC SURGERY
POCATELLO, IDAHO

One day, I got a surprising call from Dr. Moulton, a veterinarian in the small town of Blackfoot, Idaho. He wanted to consult about a patient of his, a puppy named Max.

Max was a 12-week-old Yorkshire terrier. He was the runt of his litter, and he had a fatal heart defect. It was a heart defect that you sometimes see in babies, so at the suggestion of a mutual friend, Dr. Moulton had called me.

Usually, Dr. Moulton said, he wouldn't try to save a puppy with such a severe heart problem. But Max was different.

Max's owner was a boy named Tristan, the son of a cousin of Dr. Moulton's. Six-year-old Tristan suffered from spinal muscular atrophy, a degenerative disease that attacks nerve cells in the spinal cord. Tristan was in a wheelchair and needed care around the clock. He had lived longer than his doctors had predicted, but it was a continual battle, with never-ending doctors' appointments and therapy sessions.

Tristan's parents wanted their son to have a loving companion, so they took him to pick out a puppy. Tristan's eyes lit up when he saw Max. "He's the smallest one, just like me!" he told his parents.

It was love at first sight for Tristan and Max, and they became inseparable. But only a few weeks after they adopted the puppy, Dr. Moulton discovered the heart defect.

Hearing all this, I had tears in my eyes.

Dr. Moulton went on to say that he had consulted with a hospital in Seattle that had agreed to do the surgery, but that it would cost thousands of dollars. No one in the family had that kind of money. Still, Dr. Moulton was determined to help his family.

"I've operated on a ferret," he said, "and I've dealt with an ectopic pregnancy in a chicken, but this surgery is way beyond my experience. Can you help me?"

Of course I said I'd help, although I'd never operated on a dog before.

Then, Dr. Moulton told me something that really floored me— Max weighed just a little over one pound. Holy smokes! All I could think was how huge my equipment would be next to this little guy!

My nurse and physician's assistant thought I was kidding when I told them about Max. But they gladly agreed to accompany me and assist with the surgery.

On the day of the surgery, we drove down to Dr. Moulton's clinic in Blackfoot. We put the puppy to sleep, and then separated his tiny rib cage and got to work on his heart. The pup's heart was tiny, no larger than a gum ball. But everything went well, and within an hour we had repaired the heart and closed him back up. In just a few hours, Max was awake and up on all fours, doing just fine.

I later went to meet Tristan and his parents at his home. Believe me, it was worth the world to me to see him together with Max and to hear him say, "Thank you, doctor, for saving my dog's life!"

Dr. Jacob DeLaRosa is a cardiothoracic surgeon and chief of cardiovascular and thoracic surgery at Idaho State University, Portneuf Medical Center in Pocatello, Idaho. Dr. DeLaRosa gained national attention for donating his time to save Max's life; he was featured in People *magazine ("Operation Yorkie," May 24, 2010) and on* The Wendy Williams Show *("Miracle Worker," May 28, 2010).*

41

THE FACE OF A FRIEND

PAUL O. JONES, MD, FAAFP

FAMILY MEDICINE

NAPLES, FLORIDA

He heals the brokenhearted and binds up their wounds....
Great is our Lord, and mighty in power.

PSALM 147:3,5

During my residency training at BayFront Medical Center in St.
Petersburg, I had the long shifts in the hospital that any resident has,
but I also began to see patients as a family practitioner.

One of my patients was Sofia, a 16-year-old girl who was struggling with depression. She received counseling while I treated her
with medication. She was underweight and couldn't seem to maintain
any weight she did gain. I monitored her weight and counseled her in
nutrition. We celebrated each pound she managed to gain. She was
really working hard to get well. We developed a good doctor-patient
relationship over the two years she came to me.

One night, I was on call at the emergency room when a young
woman was wheeled in on a gurney. She had been shot in the abdomen. I looked at her face and my heart sank. It was Sofia.

Sofia had been out with a group of friends that night, walking the pier. At the time, the crack epidemic had hit the city big time and gangs of louts high on drugs hung out there. On this night, security guards had kicked a group of them out. Angry and irrational, they decided to return—this time with guns. They fired off a few shots and one of them hit Sofia.

I called the trauma surgeon over. We lifted Sofia onto the operating table and began to work on her. The bullet had lacerated her liver, and she was suffering from heavy internal bleeding. We worked for four hours to stop the bleeding.

Despite our efforts, the blood continued to ooze from the abdominal area. Sofia had gone into what's called disseminated intravascular coagulation. Her body's blood-clotting mechanism was failing.

At about 4 A.M., Sofia died on the operating table.

I went out into the waiting room to face Sofia's family. Families waiting for news of their loved ones can sense the outcome just by looking at your face. Sofia's family knew right away, without my saying a word.

Even as they clung together for strength, struggling in the first moments of their grief, Sofia's parents and siblings hugged and kissed me. They thanked me for doing what I could for Sofia.

While we could not save Sofia, I knew then that I had made a difference for her. When Sofia was wheeled in, she was semi-conscious, fading in and out. Yet when she saw my face, she recognized me, and I saw her breathe a sigh of relief.

I am so thankful that I was on call that night. If I had not been, Sofia and her family would have been surrounded by strangers. Not only that, but because I was there, I knew—and the family knew—that we had done everything we could. It gave the family a measure of peace. It gave *me* a measure of peace. It confirmed for me my calling as a doctor—as one who brings healing into even the most devastating of life's events.

Dr. Paul O. Jones practices family medicine in his Naples, Florida, concierge practice and is a Fellow in the American Academy of Family Physicians. A native of Kingston, Jamaica, he came to the United States in 1978, where he pursued his medical studies. He has served two terms as chairman of the Department of Family Medicine at NCH Healthcare System and is currently president of the NCH medical staff. Dr. Jones volunteers at the Neighborhood Health Clinic in Naples and, along with other members of the Rotary Club of Naples North, he worked on construction of the Caribbean Christian Center for the Deaf in Jamaica. He and his wife, Susan, live in Naples and have four children, Stephanie, Andrew, Nathan, and Juno.

42

EARTHQUAKE IN HAITI

On January 12, 2010, a catastrophic earthquake registering 7.0 on the Richter scale struck southern Haiti 16 miles west of the capital of Port-au-Prince. Millions of people were killed, maimed, or left homeless by the quake. Many countries aided the relief effort by sending rescuers, funds, food and water, medical teams, and building crews. Drs. Peggy Sarjeant and Clydette Powell volunteered in the days and weeks following the earthquake.

GOD'S CELL PHONE

PEGGY SARJEANT, MD

PEDIATRIC MEDICINE

SEATTLE, WASHINGTON

Hundreds of maimed and crushed people lay on bare mattresses in the concrete rooms of the orphanage.

The compound was perched on a hot, wind-swept hillside above Étang Saumâtre, Haiti's largest lake. The injured had been transported from Port-au-Prince in freight trucks, the beds of pickup trucks, the trunks of cars. Their stumps, mangled bones, and broken spines were supported by sheets of cardboard, rough wooden planks, and doors.

My friend, Vicki, an emergency medicine physician, was among the first to arrive in Haiti after the earthquake. She had nearly singlehandedly set up this field hospital outside Jimaní, Dominican Republic, two miles from the Haitian border. I arrived five days later.

The first aftershock occurred at sunset on my third evening in Jimaní. All two hundred patients and their surviving family members ran, hobbled, crawled, even jumped from the V-shaped concrete building, screaming as the earth heaved beneath us. Those who couldn't move were carried. Outside, women keened, children cried, and men jostled to claim space in the dirt yard for their sick and injured.

The building was unscathed, but following two more aftershocks, the Haitians refused to re-enter it. By morning, a tent city had sprung up in the yard. The able-bodied had reassembled the orphanage's few steel bed frames, planted sticks and scrap lumber in the hardpan earth, and canopied the makeshift structures with bed sheets and cardboard to shelter the injured from the scorching sun. Thereafter all care, except for the amputations that were performed in the ill-equipped ORs inside the building, was delivered in the yard.

By day, downdraft from a constant stream of helicopters shredded the Haitians' shelters. These air-evacs had capacity only for the most gravely injured—the severely burned, the quadriplegics, the crushed infants. By night, our medical team started IVs, administered antibiotics, and changed wound dressings on our knees, in the dirt, our patients illuminated only by our headlamps.

One afternoon I was aroused from my fitful daytime sleep. "Vicki needs you," the young man said. "Now."

Inside the compound, the air was close and the heat wilting. The tent city was nearly impossible to navigate. People had combined their flimsy havens into larger, more durable shelters, and the pathways between had disappeared. I finally found Vicki in the center of the camp, wearing a broad-brimmed canvas hat, surrounded by a crowd of Haitians.

Vicki turned to me. "We need to choose ten," she said. "Just ten."

The head of our relief organization had arranged for two helicopters to transport ten injured children and their family members to the organization's outpatient facility deeper inside the Dominican Republic.

"They cannot be so sick they need care in a full-service hospital," Vicki said. "Look for healthy kids with limbs we can save or amputation stumps our surgeons can improve."

"Only ten?" I said. We were surrounded by a sea of mutilated children.

Vicki nodded. "You know the kids better than I do," she said. "Hurry! The helicopters land in twenty minutes."

At that moment, Jay appeared. Jay had established himself as coordinator of air evacuations. The day before, I had pleaded with Jay to transport Nadia, a newly paraplegic woman I had found lying on the door that had been ripped from her house; Nadia had a bedsore eroded through to her pelvic bone. Jay had laughed at me.

Now, Jay was livid, and Vicki was his target. He ranted that she had overstepped her authority, she had not cleared the evacuation with him, and she had gone over the heads of the camp "administration." He hurled expletives and derogatory references to her character. "You do not have the right to make a decision to transport anyone off the premises!" Jay shouted.

My friend Vicki sat among the crowd of Haitians and simply smiled.

Jay stood up. He thrust his index finger in Vicki's face. "How did this happen?" he demanded.

Vicki swept off her hat and shrugged. "It's the hand of God," she said.

Jay thrust his index finger once more toward Vicki's face. "Maybe so," Jay nearly spat. "But God doesn't have a cell phone."

Vicki turned to me. "I have two children in mind," she said. "You find eight. Go!" Jay turned his back and walked away.

I found the first three right away, because they were immobile. Antoine and Sandrine both had femur fractures, stabilized in hip spica casts now soiled with urine and feces. Three-year-old John, his right buttock and thigh stripped of flesh, lay with his mother on the pavement.

And then it was as if God really *did* have a cell phone. Within minutes I found the others in every far corner of the compound.

Kevin, the stitches across his leg stump hanging in shreds, with bits of fat and muscle oozing from the open wound. Luciano, his arm lopped off at the shoulder by falling cinder blocks. Stanley, a young teen with a compound fracture of the left leg, and his right hand partially amputated. Silo, his crushed leg filleted by the surgeons to keep the pressure of massive swelling from destroying the tissue. Mikeline, her right arm traumatically amputated by falling debris, her thigh skinned like a deer carcass.

Choosing was a heartbreaking task. There were so many others.

By sunset, the helicopters still had not arrived. The families gathered around the orphanage gate, and Vicki prepared them for one more night in the open. Vicki and I slept fitfully, wondering if the families would lose their trust and disperse.

But sunrise found everyone assembled. The kids' hair was combed, and their faces washed. Parents donned clean dresses and creased khakis pulled from the trash bags that held their only belongings.

I began tagging the parents and children to make sure we didn't leave anyone behind. Vicki was glued to her cell phone, trying to find out from someone, somewhere, if the air-evac was still a go.

And then Jay appeared, followed by his cohort, Dr. Rhoda.

Dr. Rhoda held up her hand, as if she were a police officer forbidding me to cross the street.

"I just heard, from the *highest authority*," she said, "that this operation is off!"

The highest authority? I wondered whom she could possibly mean. As far as I could tell, no human being was in charge.

Inexplicably, I responded, "Well, *I* heard this morning, from the *highest authority*, that this operation is on!"

At that moment, two Blackhawk helicopters appeared over Étang Saumâtre. I turned away from Jay and Dr. Rhoda and headed for the makeshift helipad. Thirty minutes later, the injured children and their desperate parents were lifted high above the chaos of Jimaní, on their way to hope and help.

I wonder sometimes how well-meaning people, united in their commitment to help, can be so divisive. I wonder, too, about all the children we left behind. Our time on this earth is often difficult to navigate, and grief seems sometimes more prevalent than joy. But even in the worst of times, there is hope. And this time, there was someone on the other end of a cell phone that for a few families made all the difference in the world.

Dr. Peggy Sarjeant practiced general pediatrics in Seattle, Washington, for 20 years. She volunteered with Children of the Nations as a first responder to the Haiti earthquake in January 2010. She has also worked in Kenya, both in hospitals and in the bush. Dr. Sarjeant's essay about the stresses of practicing medicine, "A Fire, Deliberately Set," appeared in Becoming a Doctor: From Student to Specialist, Doctor-Writers Share Their Experiences *(W.W. Norton, 2010) and her short story "Looking for Oxygen" won an award from the Pacific Northwest Writers Association. Her short fiction has appeared in* Cutthroat *and* The Portland Review. *Dr. Sarjeant lives in Seattle, Washington, with her husband and two young adult children.*

A MOMENT OF COMFORT

CLYDETTE POWELL, MD, MPH, FAAP

PEDIATRICS, CHILD NEUROLOGY

AND PUBLIC HEALTH

WASHINGTON, DC

Dr. Powell served aboard the military hospital ship USNS Comfort *following the earthquake. She worked nearly nonstop for four weeks. During this time, she wrote e-mail notes home to her mother.*

February 7

Oh, Mom, your notes sustain me. They make it possible for me to do this hard work and to reap the rewards. Today, I am of course thinking about this same day one year ago when Dad died.

No one here on the *USNS Comfort*—no one in Haiti—knows of this day's significance for me. Yet, God has placed this work before me, and it helps me with my grief to focus on his tasks.

Today, I accompanied a 10-year-old girl named Faika by helicopter from the *Comfort* to a field hospital near Haiti's border with the Dominican Republic.

Faika and her father came into our pediatric intensive care unit (PICU) on January 24. Not home when the earthquake struck, her dad was spared. But upon arriving home, he found that his wife and two of his daughters had died. Faika, his third daughter, somehow survived, with head, leg, and pelvic injuries, and was rushed to a field hospital in Port-au-Prince.

Faika developed multiple medical problems, including kidney failure and fluid in her lungs, which caused her to stop breathing and be placed on a breathing machine. Two weeks later, she was transported by helicopter to the ship's PICU, where she remained on a breathing machine for another few days.

Faika nearly died. Yet, over the course of her stay, she began to improve slowly; gradually, her kidney failure and respiratory distress resolved. She received a transfusion for marked anemia, and finally she was well enough to recognize her very grateful father.

Throughout all the uncertainty, her father quietly expressed his faith in God and his unending hope for his daughter, the only precious thing that remained to him. He had a deep faith in the Lord in the face of unimaginable tragedy.

Over the next two weeks, I followed Faika's course. Conversing in French, her father and I spoke of their circumstances and needs, but Faika remained silent, never saying a word. She was likely traumatized by all that she saw in the earthquake and in the PICU.

Today was her patient discharge day. Though not completely healed, she was ready for transfer back to the mainland. She and her dad were excited, although they were apprehensive about what awaited them. Their home and his livelihood had been completely destroyed by the quake, and they were being transferred to a place far from Port-au-Prince.

This morning, I waited with them in the ship's emergency room for her move up to the flight deck and helicopter transport out. To my surprise and delight, the air boss gave me the thumbs up to accompany Faika and her father in the helicopter.

Oh, Mom, I was thrilled! While the helicopter's rotor blades thumped loudly, they loaded Faika's litter into the bird, and then her dad and I got on board.

When we lifted off from the flight deck, Faika gripped my left hand, and in my right hand was her dad's. We became a threesome, soaring over the bay, over Haiti's capital city, and then into the rural interior, arriving some twenty minutes later at the field hospital.

The pilots told me they had another run to make, but would pick me up on their way back. "Powell, you've got 40 minutes to get your work done, because we can't wait for you at the landing zone," they warned me.

At the triage tent, we were greeted by an orthopedic surgeon from Chicago and two Creole-speaking female volunteers. The surgeon carefully removed Faika's wound dressings. He commented on how well cared for she had been on the *Comfort* and how nicely the wounds were granulating in. They began the process of admitting Faika to the field hospital.

Knowing I had just a short time until pick-up, I immediately began to explore. As I was making my way around, I heard a voice behind me.

"Clydette?!?"

I turned around, astonished to hear my name. It was my dear friend Diane!

Diane is a pediatrician and a missionary doctor in Pakistan. I had last seen her when we were working together in Southeast Asia in February 2009. Temporarily based stateside, she had volunteered to help in the Haitian relief effort. You can imagine my surprise at seeing her!

I was delighted that I could hand over Faika's care to the field hospital's only pediatrician and a trusted friend. That in itself seemed divinely orchestrated. But meeting up with Diane held an even greater personal significance for me.

Mom, it was Diane who was with me when I received the news that Dad had died! I don't know how I would have managed without her. She was an immense source of comfort in my time of grief.

All today, in the back of my head and deep in my heart, I wondered how God would address my grief. And here—when I had just minutes on the ground—he brought me to Diane, the only person in Haiti who knew of and had experienced my own personal earthquake 365 days ago!

Diane and I hugged hard and long. I brought her to Faika's bed and introduced her to my patient and her father. Forty minutes later, the noise of thumping blades announced the arrival of my ride back to the ship. I enjoyed last hugs with Faika and her dad, and finally Diane, and then I ran for the landing zone.

As I jumped on board the helicopter, I found myself wishing Dad could have witnessed the events of the day. Then, with tears of both joy and sorrow, I realized that, of course, he had seen everything—he is watching me from the best seat in the house!

Dr. Clydette Powell serves as a medical officer for the U.S. Agency for International Development (USAID) in Washington, D.C. Her work focuses on TB/HIV, primarily in Asia and Africa, and the health consequences of human trafficking. She has a medical degree from The Johns Hopkins School of Medicine, and a master's in Public Health from UCLA. She is board-certified in pediatrics, child neurology, and preventive medicine/public health. She works part-time as a child neurologist at Children's National Medical Center in Washington, D.C. "A Moment of Comfort" was published as "The Providence of the Comfort: Letters from Haiti" and adapted with permission from Today's Christian Doctor *(Winter, 2010), a publication of the Christian Medical and Dental Associations.*

43

A Timely Friend

Jeremy Gabrysch, MD
Emergency Medicine
Austin, Texas

Whether you turn to the right or to the left,
your ears shall hear a word behind you, saying,
"This is the way; walk in it."

Isaiah 30:21

My first trip to Africa didn't go so well. A group of college students were going on a mission trip to Sudan, and they were looking for a doctor to accompany them.

I think it was actually the parents who wanted a doctor along—the group was going to a remote area, so they wanted the comfort of knowing a doctor would be available if needed. In reality, I don't know how much of a comfort I was. I was barely older than the students myself.

My wife and I both went on the trip. It was Christina's first mission trip, and it was a hard trip for both of us. We were in the jungle, sleeping in tents on the ground, and eating strange foods. We ate goat—a lot of goat!—every part of the goat, including goat liver. On top of that, I developed a high fever and was sidelined for two days.

When we got back I thought, *Okay, so Africa's a stretch*. Still, I was convinced that God wanted me in full-time medical ministry somewhere. I speak Spanish, and I'd taken several mission trips to Mexico, so I was pretty sure that God wanted me in a Spanish-speaking country anyway.

But after we returned from Sudan, I watched a video one of the team members had made of the trip, and I felt a strange tugging at my heart. *Maybe God is calling us to Africa*, I thought.

For the next five years, I led trips to South Sudan to do health and community development work. But we weren't just Angelina Jolie and Brad Pitt over there—for me, it had to be more than that. I tried to help people think about why God had us there. I wanted us to be open to what God would have for us, how he might want to change our lives.

So, on these mission trips, I wasn't thinking only about what I was doing for someone else—I was thinking about what God was doing in my own heart. Because of the trips, I began to wonder whether God might be leading Christina and me to Sudan as missionaries.

At that time, we began to consider adopting a child. Christina and I planned to both adopt and have biological children. We looked at Sudan first, but adoptions weren't viable there, so we looked east to Ethiopia. It wasn't Sudan, but we thought, *Well, close enough.*

Ethiopia is a poor country. Families often live on less than a dollar a day. Because of the poverty, many children are left at orphanages. Families have no choice—they just can't afford to feed their children. We were blessed to adopt our son Nate from an orphanage when he was eight months old.

While we were in Ethiopia for the adoption, Christina and I took a side trip to the city of Soddo to check out the Christian hospital and orphanage there. We came back pretty sure that we could see ourselves living there. Maybe God *was* calling us to Ethiopia. We started to plan for the move.

Because of the mission trips and the trip to Ethiopia to complete Nate's adoption, I became convicted that I wasn't serving the underserved in my own community. Sure, in an emergency room you treat people from all strata of society, but it's not the same. In the teeth of the crisis, you don't have time to really listen to your patients or help them in any way other than to address the situation at hand.

I learned that there was a volunteer health clinic down the street from my hospital that treated patients for a minimal fee three nights a week. I started volunteering once a month, and I found it extremely rewarding. It was nice to have time to sit with patients, to talk with them and pray with them, all without the bustle of the ER.

Well, one night at the clinic a young man came in for treatment. He was a refugee who had just arrived in America three days earlier. I knew right away from his face and from his name—Theodros—that he was Ethiopian!

Theodros was diabetic. He had been diligent about taking his medicine in Ethiopia and didn't want to run out of it here in the States. I fixed him up with the prescription he needed.

Theodros was surprised that I could identify him as Ethiopian, and was thrilled to learn that I had a son from Ethiopia. I proudly showed him Nate's picture in my wallet. But he was perplexed when I told him that we were planning to move to Ethiopia. He had spent eight years on a waiting list desperate to leave Ethiopia for the opportunity to live in America. Theodros is a Christian, but even so, he told me, "That's crazy!"

Already, Theodros had plugged into the Ethiopian community, living with several other Ethiopian men and attending an Ethiopian church. But of course, he needed a job, among many other things.

Theodros and I became friends. Teddy, as we now call him, met my family, and we started going to eat at an Ethiopian restaurant together. I helped him navigate the complexities of American life. For someone new to the United States, even a trip to the grocery story is scary—17 kinds of apples, 70 kinds of breakfast cereal! I helped him get a job, his own apartment, a driver's license, and a car. We would meet at a coffee shop a few times a week and go over help-wanted and classified ads. I helped him submit resumes online and went to used car lots with him to kick the tires.

In return, Teddy has taught us all about Ethiopian culture. He can answer our most confused questions: How does the country's entry visa work again? How much does that item cost in your currency?

But, to me, the best thing about our friendship has to do with language. Amharic, the language that Ethiopians speak, is one of the most difficult languages in the world to learn. It has sounds that we just don't have in English. Christina and I intended to learn Amharic after we moved to Ethiopia. But Teddy made it possible for us to start learning right away! We've had regular language lessons with him and are continuing even now as we prepare for our big move overseas.

God ordained our friendship with Teddy at just the right time, and for a unique purpose. He had our meeting at the clinic planned all along. When we adopted our son from Ethiopia, we prayed that God would send us connections to his home country, both for Nate's sake and our own. Teddy's friendship was an answer to that prayer.

Dr. Jeremy Gabrysch is a board-certified emergency room physician for Emergency Service Partners based in Austin, Texas. He and his wife, Christina, are preparing to live in Soddo, Ethiopia, where Dr. Gabrysch will work at Soddo Christian Hospital under the auspices of the Evangelical Free Church's ReachGlobal mission agency. The couple has a son, Nate, and a daughter, Taylor.

44

BLESSINGS FROM BONDING

MICHAEL O'CALLAGHAN, DDS

FAMILY DENTISTRY

ALLEGAN, MICHIGAN

Gently, I put my hand over hers. I smiled at her and said in English, "Hi. My name is Dr. Mike. I am a dentist, and I have come all the way to Inner Mongolia to help fix your teeth. The reason I do this is because my God, Jesus Christ, loves me and has blessed me. I want to share His love and blessings with others."

Li, my translator on this mission trip, began to translate my comments into Mandarin, and I looked into the eyes of this middle-aged woman. As the message unfolded, my patient looked nervously around the room, and her body stiffened. Mine was a message that could get her in deep trouble in this country. The warm expression on her face altered suddenly. She shut down and shrank from my touch.

Li, a godly woman who is both a gifted translator and an evangelist, glanced at me. I knew that I should say no more. I had been advised that any evangelizing beyond what I had already said could endanger my colleagues and patients. It was my job just to begin providing the dental care this woman had waited hours in line for at this small and remote community health clinic.

I guess you can't risk hearing about how much our Lord loves you, I thought to myself. *It will be our job to show you his love.* And so I began.

The Mongolian woman asked us to fix her two upper front teeth. Both were fractured and marred by large, black decayed areas. It was a perfect case for mission dentistry—not too complex and no root canals needed. Sometimes, mission dentists have to simply pull teeth in situations like this, but I had lugged along an extensive array of portable equipment for just such cases.

With the help of my assistants, we were able to place bonded tooth-colored resin fillings that blended into the woman's remaining natural teeth. Even with my equipment, the work took about 90 minutes to complete, more time than it would have taken in the States. When we were done, you could hardly tell the woman's teeth had ever been broken or decayed.

As we finished up, I grabbed the hand-held mirror that I'd brought along with me and handed it to her. She stared at her reflection and beamed with joy. She turned to me and smiled broadly. Then, she placed her hand on mine and, in Mandarin, said to me, "Now, tell me about this Jesus."

Wow, was I shocked! Yes, I had prayed that God would use our frail mortal efforts to sovereignly draw people into his family of faith. And I always believe that God will work, because I know that he uses everything for his glory. But, truthfully, I never expected to see any results from this day until I got to heaven.

While my assistant and I waited, Li presented the gospel to this delightful woman. We watched, listened, and silently prayed for about twenty minutes as Li and our patient conversed back and forth. Then Li smiled at us and said, "She wants to become a Christian."

Li prayed with her and our patient became our sister in the Lord that day. The slow, laborious process of restorative dentistry had given her time to consider our Lord Jesus Christ. I thank God for the privilege of using our efforts to bring this dear woman to a saving faith in him. I will see her again in heaven, and we will not need a translator then. We will have all eternity to speak of how God was faithful. Such blessings are treasures in heaven!

Dr. Michael O'Callaghan has practiced dentistry since 1981 and is in family practice in Allegan, Michigan. Since 2005, he has been on a dozen mission trips with Global Health Outreach, a ministry of the Christian Medical and Dental Associations, and he now heads up GHO medical mission teams. On his trips, he has been to Nicaragua, El Salvador, Liberia, Mexico, Cambodia, Haiti, China, and India. He and his wife, Margaret, have three grown children.

45

A DYING WISH

TIMOTHY HUTTON, MD

FAMILY MEDICINE

ST. GEORGE, ONTARIO

Of one thing I am certain; the body is not the measure of healing,

peace is the measure.

PHYLLIS MCGINLEY

In the twenty years of my solo family practice, patients have occasionally fainted or had a seizure in my office, but only once did someone actually die in my waiting room.

Bill was in his early 80s and suffered from progressive congestive heart failure. He was adamant that he did not want to go to the hospital for treatment, possibly because he did not want to endure unpleasant treatment, or perhaps he feared he would die while hospitalized. He had told me clearly that he did not want to die in a hospital.

I managed Bill's declining health as best I could, in the way that he wanted. I monitored him frequently at my office and gave him medicine to ease his symptoms and difficulty with breathing. I kept an eye on his cholesterol, not because I felt it was an issue, but because he was concerned about it.

One busy Monday morning, Bill's daughter called my office. The nurse who answered my phone was there, but she was helping another caller, so the daughter left a message asking whether she could bring him in. If so, she asked, would we have a wheelchair that she could use to get her father from the car into the office.

Before my nurse could return the call, Bill and his daughter showed up at the front door. We did not have a wheelchair, but the front entrance was just two steps from the driveway and a waiting room chair was only four steps from the front door. Bill's daughter began the laborious process of getting Bill in the front door.

As she was in the process of helping her father to a seat, Bill collapsed on the waiting room floor.

My nurse immediately called 911 and summoned me from the back office. While I ran to Bill and his daughter, the nurse quickly escorted other patients from the waiting room into a back room.

In the quiet of the empty waiting room, I assessed the situation. Bill was unconscious and barely breathing. I knew right away that in order to live, he would require resuscitation.

"Should I try to revive your father if he doesn't start breathing better soon, or should I let him go peacefully?" I asked the daughter, who was at his side on the floor.

This is a tricky question to ask. It can be hard for children, even as adults, to separate what they know is good for a parent, or what they dearly want for a parent, from what the parent actually wants.

In Bill's case, he had made it clear to his daughter and to me that he did not want to die in a hospital. Yet, he had also told his daughter that he did not want to die at home. That didn't leave many options. Perhaps he was simply afraid of dying.

Knowing his wishes, the daughter answered right away, without hesitation, that she would prefer her father not undergo any attempts at resuscitation, not even CPR.

So, I sat on the floor with Bill and his daughter as he quietly took his last breaths.

When the ambulance arrived a few minutes later, I excused myself to meet them outside. When a patient has arrested, EMTs will almost always try to resuscitate. I asked tactfully whether this time, due to the family's wishes, they could forego their obligation. They said they could, as long as I was willing to sign a death certificate. And so I did.

Most people do not object to being taken to the hospital. But the situation is rarely as dire as it was for Bill. Families usually have some time to come to decisions about treatment and palliative care. But you can't force patients to do something that you believe will extend their lives. Although this event made me sad, I was glad I could help Bill achieve what he wanted, a peaceful death, neither at home nor in the hospital.

Dr. Timothy Hutton has had a family medicine practice in St. George, Ontario, since 1990. He completed his premed training at Houghton College, New York, graduated from the University of Rochester School of Medicine and Dentistry, and completed a family medicine residency at McMaster University in Hamilton, Ontario. He and his wife, Sue, have two grown children, Heather and Alastair, and one son, Andrew, still at home.

46

SAFE WITH GOD

STEPHANIE WELLINGTON, MD

NEONATOLOGY

NEW YORK, NEW YORK

Hope is the feeling you have
that the feeling you have isn't permanent.

JEAN KERR

Elena gave birth to premature twins at our hospital. She had great difficulty getting pregnant, and she had been ecstatic about the babies.

But she went into labor and delivered after just 25 weeks, and the babies were tiny. At 835 grams, one weighed close to two pounds, but the other, at 560 grams, was just over a pound. They were both boys.

Both babies needed supportive care, but the smaller boy struggled more. A premature baby's airways are narrow, so his breathing was shallow, and he struggled for breath. He was lethargic and showed little movement.

After the birth, Elena and her husband were brought up to the neonatal intensive care unit to be with their babies. Soon, the smaller baby's heart rate began to drop. We did everything we could for him, but before the day was out, he coded and could not be resuscitated. Elena and her husband were at the baby's side when he died.

We left the couple alone with their grief. Elena held the tiny boy, and she and her husband wept together. She had a hard time letting the baby go, and later she asked to be taken to the morgue to see him again.

In the intimacy of the neonatal care unit, we got to know Elena and her family over the next few months as we cared for the surviving baby. He remained on a ventilator for a long time. He had surgery to place a tracheostomy tube, so we could maintain his airway. He suffered many setbacks, including sepsis and gastroesophageal reflux, which would cause his heart rate to drop dangerously. Feeding was a continual challenge.

It was an emotional time for the family. Elena was often discouraged as she weathered the ups and downs.

"When is this all going to end? When will we get to go home?" she'd ask. "Every time I try to enjoy my baby, there is always a setback."

On top of that, Elena's grief for her dead child also overwhelmed her at times. She felt well supported by her husband, but she often had to be strong for him. He wasn't very verbal about their loss, and he hadn't been able to visit the baby's graveside with her.

Although Elena was a nurse and worked among caring people, sometimes even her co-workers didn't know what to say. And, while her own family expressed sympathy and understanding, she was beginning to feel pressure from her husband's family to get on with her life.

"I think they just want me to stop grieving and cherish what I have," she said through her tears one day. "And maybe they're right. Maybe I should be grateful. It's just hard to be, sometimes."

Through working with families in the NICU, I've found that one of the best ways I can support them is simply to listen. I gave Elena my full attention and heard her out whenever she was struggling.

Some days, her shoulders were slumped and I could see she'd been crying, but I didn't turn away. "Not such a good day today, is it, Mom?" I'd ask softly. Other days, she was more animated and sometimes even smiling.

The surviving twin was in the NICU for five months, but finally the day came when he was ready to go home. He weighed just over seven pounds, and his breathing and feeding problems had resolved themselves. His discharge was right before Mother's Day, and I was happy the family would all be together for that day. Elena was happy, too.

"I don't think I will ever understand why my baby died," she told me. "I'm not sure there is a reason. But I know that he's out of pain now, and I know he's safe with God."

Elena's words were hard won, and I was proud of her. Elena and her baby have returned to visit us since that day. The baby is growing, and both mom and baby look happy. I feel they are in a good place.

While our culture says that a birth is supposed to be a joyous event, it isn't always experienced that way. Families in the NICU suffer from emotional turmoil that is very similar to post-traumatic stress. I find it tremendously rewarding to help moms and dads nurture themselves back to a place of calm and inner peace.

Dr. Stephanie Wellington has more than ten years' experience as a physician in neonatal intensive care units. Currently, she practices at Bellevue Hospital in Manhattan. She is also a postpartum neonatal life coach who helps parents with the stresses and heartaches of caring for premature or sick infants. She has two children, Basil and Mackenzie.

47

THE GIFT OF LAUGHTER

FOLAKE TAYLOR, MD
INTERNAL MEDICINE
DAWSONVILLE, GEORGIA

A cheerful heart is good medicine,
but a crushed spirit dries up the bones.

PROVERBS 17:22

My favorite column in *Reader's Digest* is "Laughter, The Best
Medicine." To me, laughing is serious business. Laughter lowers
blood pressure, reduces stress hormones, increases muscle flexion,
and boosts immune function. Besides—I just love to laugh.

I started out as a country doctor in Georgia. My patients gave
me plenty of opportunity to laugh. There was Ron, the patient who
handed us a few ounces of Mountain Dew as a urine sample for his
drug screening. He was sure it would test just fine! And Mr. Brown,
the avid hunter who paid me in cuts of venison. Deer burger, deer
stew meat, deer sausage—you name it, we ate it.

One patient in particular always brought a smile to my face. Becky
was witty and intelligent, quick with a joke and brimming with
funny stories.

The thing is, Becky's life was pretty bad. She was a white woman who had married an African American man, and they had two biracial children, which had turned her into the family's black sheep. She suffered endlessly from racial intolerance. She was divorced and raising the children on her own, and her teenage daughter was pregnant.

Becky had almost too many health challenges to count. She weighed about 350 pounds and suffered from diabetes, hypertension, and chronic low back pain. On top of that, she was bipolar, so even though she was trying to get her health problems under control, she was hampered by the emotional swings of the bipolar disorder.

Although Becky faithfully kept her monthly appointments with me, she frequently landed in the emergency room between visits. Her diabetes was so out of control that her endocrinologist had put her on an insulin pump and even that didn't keep her out of the hospital. She often slipped into a diabetic coma, sometimes for days on end. She was a regular at the ICU. It had become her normal.

Becky was so sick that she could no longer work. And, just when it seemed that things couldn't get any worse, she lost her health coverage.

Not even these trials could dampen Becky's spirit. She told endless stories of her past life—a time when she lived, worked, and was able to move around like everybody else—a time when she, in her own words, didn't weigh a ton.

One afternoon, toward the end of the day, I entered the exam room to find Becky sitting in the corner, reading. A smile spread across my face. We chatted—and laughed—for a few minutes.

I began Becky's exam, checking her heart and other body systems. Then I had her lie down on the exam table so I could do an abdominal exam and a straight leg raise. With the leg raise, I could check on the nature and severity of her back pain.

When the exam was finished, I told Becky she could sit up. As she struggled to push herself up from the table, I stretched out my hand to help her, grabbing her hand in an arm wrestling pose.

"Oh, no, you don't, Dr. Taylor!" she yelled at me, pulling back her hand.

I was taken aback by her forcefulness, wondering what on earth I had done to offend her.

"I'm just trying to help you up, Becky," I explained, a little meekly. She would have none of it.

"Doc, if I break your back, I won't have a doctor to come to next month!" she quipped. "I need *you* to be healthy!"

We both broke out into loud fits of laughter.

Now that I have moved on from my country practice, I miss Becky. I often think about her and wonder how she is doing. But I know what she did for me. She made me laugh. I have my own health struggles, so when patients are able to laugh through their physical and emotional trials, and make others laugh to boot, it reminds me that I can laugh my way through anything, too.

That is just one of the many things that my patients do for me. They keep me laughing, and they help me to put things in perspective in life. May we never lose the ability to laugh. It is a great gift from above—a very precious gift.

Dr. Folake Taylor is a board-certified internist practicing primary care in Dawsonville, Georgia, a suburb of Atlanta. She was born in the United Kingdom to Nigerian parents and has lived in the United States since 2000.

She is the author of The Only Way is Up: The Journey of an Immigrant *(Arrabon Publishing, 2010). She and her husband, Layi, are the parents of a daughter, Jordan.*

48

WHO DO YOU TRUST?

DANIEL BENEDICK, MD

FAMILY MEDICINE

SHELL, ECUADOR

Here at Hospital Vozandes del Oriente in Shell, Ecuador, we take turns manning the hospital while other doctors take the outpatient clinic. A week ago I had a crazy turn as the hospital doc.

I'd already admitted two really sick older gentlemen to the hospital when we received a phone call that a very sick little girl was on the way. She had been seen in an outlying clinic, and her story was not entirely clear. From what we could gather, Valentina was nine years old and had been having seizures. Her mother had sent her to school that day, apparently normal other than a cough and a sore throat.

At some point in their children's school years, many parents get a call from the school nurse telling them to come pick up their child: "She's fallen off the jungle gym and hit her head," or "He's been in a fight on the playground, and he's a little banged up." Well, my patient's mother received a call from the school, but in this case the teacher said, "Come and get your daughter now, because she is dying."

I examined Valentina in the emergency room, while her mother looked on. She was unconscious, but responding slightly to pain. She was moving her arm in a strange way that appeared to be what we call decerebrate posturing. That means, essentially, that the damage has reached the brainstem and the brain is dying or has already died.

In spite of the medicine we gave her to stop the seizures, Valentina seized two more times in the emergency room. We were blessed to have received the results of a CT scan that had been performed in a neighboring town, and we were able to rule out bleeding in or around her brain. We performed a lumbar puncture—a spinal tap—to evaluate the fluid around her brain, which looked normal.

Throughout the diagnostic process, the girl's mother began to cry out to God. "Lord," she said, "You know that I only have one daughter. Please spare her! I beg you!"

As she prayed, I asked if I could pray along. We prayed together for several minutes. We asked again and again for Valentina's healing and for guidance in treating her. The prayers put all of us in the room at peace.

After that, we moved her to a hospital bed and started her on supportive treatments—IV fluids, anti-seizure medicines, and acetaminophen. We gave her antibiotics, too, because she had reportedly been having fevers, and we wanted to treat her for meningitis, just in case.

But we still didn't know what was wrong with her. Infection? Accidental poisoning? Whatever the case was, she didn't seem to be waking up.

About an hour after Valentina was placed in a hospital bed, we received a request from her parents: "Could we please take our daughter out of the hospital for an hour or two? We'd like to take her over to the shaman to see if he can heal her."

Now, a shaman is a traditional healer. Many of them practice in our area, and they typically call upon evil forces. They claim to be mediums to the spiritual realm and rely on curses, the "evil eye," and other fear-invoking rituals and dances. In Ecuador, their healing arsenal includes plants, eggs, guinea pigs, drugs, and cigarette smoke.

As a parent, I know that I would do almost anything for my child. However, Valentina's parents, after having just prayed to the one true God, now wanted to turn for help to Satan.

I suspected Valentina's father was pressuring his wife to see the shaman. So I went into Valentina's room and pleaded with them.

"Who do you trust?" I asked them. "Do you trust the power of God or the power of the shaman? I encourage you to trust in God alone."

With their child's life on the line, the parents decided to keep their daughter in the hospital. They maintained their trust in God and in their child's doctors—who were, of course, relying heavily on God.

Over the next two days, my sweet little patient gradually awoke from her unconscious state. On the third day, she was completely back to normal. To this day, we don't know what was wrong with her.

The Lord always answers prayers in the best possible way, although they're not always answered in the way that we think is best. In the Gospels, Jesus heals a blind man and then tells him, "Your faith has healed you."

God wants to do marvelous things through us on this earth. Valentina's family will always have this testimony about how their daughter was healed through God's power, because they were willing to put their trust in him alone. Praise him for his healing touch!

*Dr. Daniel Benedick served as a family practitioner with the World
Medical Mission of Samaritan's Purse in Shell, Ecuador, for two years.
He and his wife, Kristina, have three children, Caleb, Jael, and Anna.
"Who Do You Trust?" is excerpted with permission from the family's blog,*
Benedicks in Ecuador *(www.benedicks4jesus.blogspot.com).*

49

Me, the Doctor

Roxanne Richards, MD
Lt. Cmdr., U.S. Navy (Ret.)
Emergency Medicine
Portage, Wisconsin

Sometimes doctors get stuck in an emotional disconnect. They look at a patient as The Gallbladder in 604A, instead of Mrs. Hennessey with three children and five grandchildren. I understand how this happens.

I did my surgical residency training in Chicago, at a hospital that wasn't in a good part of town. Gang warfare and turf battles ensured that our emergency room was plenty busy. It was a good place to learn trauma care.

One night when I was a second-year resident, we got a call that an ambulance was coming in with a gunshot victim, a 13-year-old kid hit at close range by a bullet from a shotgun. He was an innocent bystander, hit in an exchange of gunfire between rival gangs.

The boy had been struck in the lower back. The emergency crew said they had him in military anti-shock trousers, which are designed to prevent blood from pooling in the legs and direct it back to the heart and brain.

As soon as the ambulance hit the door, we had two large-bore IVs and a central line in the boy, as well as a high-flow mask to deliver oxygen. He was able to talk at this point. But all of a sudden, the boy looked me straight in the eyes.

"Doc, I can't breathe," he said.

"Hang in there," I said. "We're going to help you now."

I never tell a patient he's going to be okay, because you don't know that. In fact, the boy stopped breathing then, and we lost his blood pressure.

Quickly, we had the boy intubated and wheeled him to the operating room. A medical student performed chest compressions along the way.

Once we got to the operating room, the scene became chaotic. The anesthesiologist is screaming, "I can't get a blood pressure!" The scrub nurses are annoyed, because they have to open up their trays and get everything in order—they're thinking about all the work it will be to clean and sterilize the instruments afterward.

The chief resident tells me to do a "stem-to-stern" incision. This is the first time I've ever been asked to do this. I take a knife and cut from the boy's sternum to the pubic bone. After that, I need to get into the abdominal cavity and take hold of the aorta and vena cava to clamp them off, put pressure on them, so the kid doesn't bleed to death.

I performed the maneuver needed to get to the aorta—it's called a Kocher procedure—but when I try to grab the aorta, it's not there. There's nothing there. I feel deeper, to where the boy's vertebrae should be, but they're gone too, completely shattered. He was probably dead even before we opened him up.

At that moment, the attending physician arrived in the operating room. He started in right away, screaming at the chief resident.

"You should never have brought him into the operating room!" he yelled. "Now it will be counted as a death on the table!"

After a few more choice words, the attending physician left. The chief resident turned calmly to a scrub nurse and told her to hand us the gut sutures. Then she quietly told me that we were going to close the holes in the boy's intestines, that she was going to teach me how to repair bowel injuries. Basically, we were going to operate on a kid who was already dead.

That moment in the operating room was surreal for me. I literally turned into a different person. It was crystal clear to me at that moment that I was functioning as a doctor. I wasn't me, Roxanne, I was me, the doctor.

This is a necessary defense mechanism for almost every doctor, and it is a good thing. It allows you to go about your job of saving lives and decreasing disability. By suturing the boy's intestines—whether he was dead or alive—I was learning a skill that I would need to have as a surgeon.

But while this ability to disconnect, to shut off your emotions, is valuable, it is also scary. I have seen surgeons who can't come back out of it. It took me about a year to process the emotions of that night. Because of instances like this, and other personal events that knocked me off my feet over the next few years, I considered leaving medicine altogether. I think almost every doctor gets to that point, drowning in a fog of exhaustion and endless work.

Eventually, I came to a place where life wasn't making any sense to me, no matter how much training or education I had. In desperation,

I began going to church with my sister-in-law. In February of 1998, I committed my life to Christ in the atrium of that church.

After that, medicine became entirely different for me. I had a whole new perspective. I can see a patient and understand that God made him who he is, and that God has a reason for bringing him to me. Maybe I can't cure a patient's diabetes, or her heart troubles, but maybe I can encourage her a little. I can fully use my skills on mission trips—you can make people in a poor country so happy just by listening to them, and maybe giving them Tylenol and some vitamins for their kids.

What a joy to practice medicine the way I believe God crafted me to work! This is the way I've always wanted to practice medicine. Now I'm me, Roxanne, *and* me, the doctor.

Dr. Roxanne Richards is a retired military and emergency room physician. During her career, she was a lieutenant commander in the U.S. Navy and the director of two emergency room departments. In retirement, she volunteers at a free clinic in Portage, Wisconsin, and provides ultrasounds for a resource pregnancy center. She and her husband, Jim Brant, take annual mission trips with their church to the Dominican Republic. They have five adult children and six grandchildren.

50

THE COST OF SERVING LIFE

JOHN FULGINITI III, MD, FACS, MA

GENERAL SURGERY

OVIEDO, FLORIDA

Surgeons must be very careful

When they take the knife!

Underneath their fine incisions

Stirs the Culprit—Life!

EMILY DICKINSON

Surgical training and practice has taught me something of the way God has ordered the universe. I have realized there is a cost to those who serve in the preservation of life. The more deeply one is involved in this endeavor, the greater the cost.

While preparing for the privilege of operating on fellow human beings, I endured physical, mental, and emotional trauma. Most people know that medical students and residents grind through thousands of hours of work and study. On top of this grueling load, they often suffer the same punishing level of verbal abuse that a soldier in boot camp does.

On my first day in the operating room as a resident, I was sent in to assist in a femoral-to-popliteal artery bypass operation. Upon entering, I saw that the operating table was raised for the taller surgeons. The scrub nurse asked me, "Would you like a stepstool, doctor?"

"He doesn't know what he wants," growled the attending surgeon, not even looking up.

"You know, you're stupid," he said. "You're stupid all day long. You're stupid from 7 A.M. to 7 P.M. From 7 P.M. to 7 A.M., you might be able to fool some, but you're still stupid."

I didn't say anything in response, but I thought, *Here we go. These are the surgeons I've always heard about.*

In a way, though, the surgeon's outburst didn't surprise me. We surgeons are a colorful lot. It takes a certain type of person to cut open another human being. It is a violent thing in many ways.

In the course of my training, I learned that sickness never takes a break—it doesn't have a 9-to-5 schedule, and so neither do we. At one point in my residency, I was charged with caring for an entire cardiac surgery intensive care unit. Patients in this kind of ICU need a lot of care. One patient had a bank of eight pumps through which his medications were being administered. During this stint, I realized how many hours there are in a week. Of the 168 hours of that week, I worked 140 hours.

As the hours in residency are long, so they are in private practice. I have often worked 24-hour shifts, many times on alternating days. If a patient requires an emergency surgery in the middle of the night, you don't cancel the surgeries scheduled for the next morning. You just keep working.

On top of all this, there is the emotional trauma of repeatedly watching people suffer and die, sometimes brutally, from disease or trauma. I've seen patients so bloated with the fluids we have given them that they don't look human anymore. Even the act of wounding someone in a surgical procedure, though undertaken to heal, has an emotional cost that cannot be denied. Oftentimes we are called on to make split-second life-and-death decisions. When a patient does not heal, but instead worsens or dies, we are in agony. We wonder: *Did that person suffer because of me?*

Our families suffer along with us. Because of my profession, my wife has spent many lonely hours. Once while I was in private practice, we were heading out the door to celebrate her birthday when my phone rang. I had to leave her there to assist my partner with an operation. When we do manage to get away on vacation, I find it hard to mentally release my patients, and I don't fully relax until it's almost time to go home. We have a family of five children whose care often falls to my wife. Families of doctors learn that other people's suffering always comes first.

Yet along with the suffering comes great privilege. Yes, there are the worldly privileges of status and financial security. But to hear the hurts and longings of another person, to enter into that through our doctor-patient relationship, that is a tremendous privilege.

It is a particular privilege to see the intricate workings of a human being made in the image of God. The first time I saw the inside of a living human, I was so excited. It was marvelous! The body is so filled with beauty. The colors in particular astound me: the bowel is pink, the omentum yellow, the liver brick red, the gall bladder anything from green to robin's egg blue, the arteries white and veins blue. Even though it wounds me to do it, to cut into a fellow human being's body and be confronted with the pulsating, colorful, astounding mystery of it all is a privilege. It is profoundly humbling. Life is so precious.

Yet I often wondered why we as physicians bother to prolong life. We all die in the end, every one of us, so what is the point? What does all my training and suffering amount to?

I have come to believe that the cost we pay reflects the value of God's gift of life. Not only has God granted us physical life, but Christ, through his death and resurrection, has offered us eternal life. Jesus paid the supreme price for this gift, a gift that is infinitely more precious than physical life. He did this for his glory but also that we could enjoy him—the source of life, goodness, beauty, and truth, forever. And, because he suffered all things, Christ is exalted above all things at the Father's right hand.

As physicians, we don't struggle to stave off our mortal enemy, death, as much as we labor to proclaim this truth of God's gift of life. In working to overcome physical death, even if temporarily, we proclaim Christ's ultimate victory over death. It is in Christ's death, resurrection, and ascension that we find meaning for our efforts, a meaning that transcends physical life. This is why I believe we undertake our admittedly frail and temporary work. This is the greatest privilege we derive from our costly service.

Dr. John Fulginiti III is a surgeon at Florida Hospital DeLand and a Fellow in the American College of Surgeons. He was a surgeon in private practice for 14 years. He holds a Master of Arts in Christian Thought at Reformed Theological Seminary in Oviedo, Florida, and has founded The Institute for Human Flourishing, a think tank that will address the idea of what it means to be a human being made in the image of God. He and his wife, Sarah, have five children, Gabriela, Renata, John, Elena, and James.

Acknowledgments

I am grateful to Leafwood Publishers for allowing me to continue the Miracles & Moments of Grace series. So many times during the writing of these books, chaplains and doctors expressed their gratitude to me for telling their stories. But it is I who am forever grateful to them for sharing their exquisite experiences with me. My thanks go once again to Leonard Allen, Gary Myers, Duane Anderson, Phil Dosa, Robyn Burwell, Ryan Self, Seth Shavers, and the dedicated team at Leafwood.

My gratitude extends to my agent, Bill Jensen, who has ably and diplomatically dissuaded me from my less inspired ideas and swiftly identified the ones worth pursuing. Without him, I wouldn't have arrived at the wonderful place in which I find myself—eager to start writing every morning and disappointed that I seem to need sleep on a regular basis.

The inspiring doctors who told me their stories for this book didn't just show up on my doorstep one morning. Several organizations and many people took me under their wing. In particular, I would like to thank the Christian Medical and Dental Associations for putting word of the book out to their members—Margie Shealy, Mandi Mooney, and Melinda Mitchell went out of their way to assist me. Jessica Toews of the DeMoss Group generously put me in touch with several doctors serving with Samaritan's Purse. Dot Boersma and Karen Fritz, MD, sent word around the medical student fellowship of Tenth Presbyterian Church in Philadelphia. And, finally, Nancy

Lascheid, RN, rallied the doctors who volunteer for the Neighborhood Health Clinic in Naples, Florida, to come to my aid.

As always, I am deeply aware of the debt of gratitude I owe to my husband, John, who supports my growing obsession with storytelling in every way imaginable. He patiently hears me out over the dinner table as I ramble on about the latest, most fantastic story I've heard. He's taken our son, Evan, on countless excursions in order to give me time to work—they've gone to more baseball games, amusement parks, and NASCAR races than I can count. John, you seem genuinely eager for me to keep writing, despite the dent my work puts in your schedule, and for that, I thank you. It's only one reason I love you, but one of many reasons you continue to amaze me.

Endnotes

Introduction

1. Martin Henry Fischer, MD, was a German-American doctor, professor, and author in the early to mid-1900s. Many of his sayings and aphorisms appear in *Fischerisms: Being a sheaf of sundry and divers utterances culled from the lectures of Martin H. Fischer, professor of physiology in the University of Cincinnati*, eds. Howard Fabing and Ray Marr (Springfield, IL: Charles C. Thomas, 1944).

2. Marc E. Agronin, MD, *How We Age: A Doctor's Journey into the Heart of Growing Old* (Cambridge, MA: Da Capo Press, 2011), 247.

3. "Bridging Medicine and Spirituality: Interview with Dr. Allen Hamilton," *SC Super Consciousness: The Voice of Human Potential* (Fall 2010, "The Spiritual Journey"): 40. Dr. Allen J. Hamilton is a neurosurgeon and author of *The Scalpel and the Soul: Encounters with Surgery, the Supernatural and the Healing Power of Hope* (New York: Tarcher, 2009).

4. Howard Markel, MD, PhD, "Patients Are Discovering 'My Doctor, the Author,'" *New York Times*, 22 August 2000. Dr. Sherwin B. Nuland is the National Book Award-winning author of *How We Die: Reflections on Life's Final Chapter* (New York: Alfred A. Knopf, 1994), among many other books.

Index

ABOUT THE AUTHOR

NANCY B. KENNEDY worked in newspapers for many years, including a stint as an editor for Dow Jones's pioneering computer news service. As a financial writer, she worked for many newspapers and magazines, including the *New York Times* and the online *Wall Street Journal*, and for the financial services firm Merrill Lynch. As an editor, she she worked for such well-respected publishing houses as Princeton University Press and Ecco Press.

Ms. Kennedy is the author of three other books in the Miracles & Moments of Grace series: *Inspiring Stories from Military Chaplains*, *Inspiring Stories from Moms*, and *Inspiring Stories of Survival*. She has also written a book of weight loss success stories titled *How We Did It*, as well as two teacher resources that combine science activities with stories of faith: *Make It, Shake It, Mix It Up* and *Even the Sound Waves Obey Him*. She writes articles and personal essays for books, magazines, and newspapers. Many can be found at her website, www.nancybkennedy.com.

Ms. Kennedy is a member of the Authors Guild. She and her husband, John, live with their son, Evan, in Hopewell, New Jersey.

A Note from the Editors

We hope you enjoy *Miracles & Moments of Grace* by
Nancy B. Kennedy, specially selected by the editors of the Books and
Inspirational Media Division of Guideposts, a nonprofit organization
that touches millions of lives every day through products and services
that inspire, encourage, help you grow in your faith, and celebrate
God's love in every aspect of your daily life.

Thank you for making a difference with your purchase of this
book, which helps fund our many outreach programs to military
personnel, prisons, hospitals, nursing homes, and educational
institutions. To learn more, visit GuidepostsFoundation.org.

We also maintain many useful and uplifting online resources. Visit
Guideposts.org to read true stories of hope and inspiration, access
OurPrayer network, sign up for free newsletters, download free e-books,
join our Facebook community, and follow our stimulating blogs.

To learn about other Guideposts publications, including the
best-selling devotional *Daily Guideposts*, go to ShopGuideposts.org,
call (800) 932-2145, or write to Guideposts, PO Box 5815, Harlan,
Iowa 51593.